Schooling without Labels

HEALTH, SOCIETY, AND POLICY

a series edited by Sheryl Ruzek and Irving Kenneth Zola

Schooling without Labels

Parents, Educators, and Inclusive Education

DOUGLAS BIKLEN

TEMPLE UNIVERSITY PRESS

Philadelphia

Temple University Press, Philadelphia 19122
Copyright © 1992 by Temple University. All rights reserved
Published 1992
Printed in the United States of America

Library of Congress Cataloging-in-Publication Data

Biklen, Douglas.
    Schooling without labels : parents, educators, and inclusive education / Douglas Biklen.
        p. cm.
    Includes bibliographical references and index.
    ISBN 0-87722-875-2.—ISBN 0-87722-876-0 (pbk.)
        1. Handicapped children—Education—United States. 2. Handicapped children—Education—Ontario—Toronto. 3. Mainstreaming in education—United States. 4. Mainstreaming in education—Ontario—Toronto. I. Title.
    LC4031.B48 1992
    371.9'0973—dc20   91-11681

TO
SARI KNOPP BIKLEN

Contents

Preface

A CRITICISM of recent developments in the field of special education is that each "advance" magnifies the authority of professionals over the lives of people with disabilities. While educational policy has often included a role for parent participation and monitoring, policy concepts such as "least restrictive environment," "individualized educational program," "continuum of services," and "multidisciplinary assessment" may actually further professional authority over the school lives of students who are designated "disabled." In the United States one result has been an increase in the number of students so labeled. But being identified as disabled and receiving increased attention has not meant necessarily that students or their parents have greater options or more control over their destinies.

A parallel development to the growth of professionalism in special education has been a social movement for integrating the education of students with and without disabilities. In part, that social movement has used the language and procedures of professional, social policy to advance its cause. For example, parents have sought professional assistance in advocating increased integration of their children into regular schools and classrooms; guarantees that their children would receive such services as sign language interpreting, speech therapy, and adaptive physical education; and the desegregation of special schools.

With parents and "their" professionals pushing for full inclusion of their children with disabilities in regular schools and classrooms, school districts and state professionals have asked a challenging question: "Are there any schools that have totally embraced the concept of integrated schooling? Are there any schools that integrate all students, no matter how severe or complex their disabilities?" While it is not clear that any school can yet claim that it has achieved total integration (any more than a given school can declare itself free of all racism or prejudice), some schools and school districts have in fact achieved integration for a very broad range of students, including those presumed to have severe disabilities.

This book asks a similar question: "Is there any place within the culture where integration already exists such that we could study it, learn from it, and apply principles from it to schools and other social settings?" As it turns out, some families have achieved "full" inclusion. And, not surprisingly, in their pursuit of family life that fully includes a child with a disability, these families present an ideology and set of practices that diverge in numerous ways from current practices and beliefs in education. Most noticeably, the parents disdain the professionalizing of their lives and their children's lives. They seek a place and experience in common with the rest of society. Instead of advocating on professional, educational grounds that their children receive certain kinds of educational services, they make simpler moral and practical arguments. The focus of this book, then, is the ways these parents think about inclusion. From them we can derive principles for reforming schools and other social institutions.

Among the people who have been helpful to me in the preparation of this book, I am particularly indebted to the parents who gave so many hours to the essential interviews and observation. Thanks to Mary Lou Accetta, Rose and Dom Galati, Susan and Bob Lehr, Linda and Kingston Till, Stan and Marthe Woronko, and the many other parents who at their request appear here under pseudonyms.

I thank also the Ministry of Education in Victoria, Australia, especially Minister Joan Kirner and staff member John Lewis. Robert Semmens and Melbourne University gave me the opportunity to make a series of presentations based on the manuscript, and the audience responses led to many useful revisions. Special thanks go to Joan Reidy for helping to organize the Victoria visit.

The readers engaged by Temple University Press made additional useful recommendations. Thanks also to Janet Francendese, senior acquisitions editor, for her advice and editing and to series editor Irving Zola for his strong encouragement and incisive criticisms.

I am grateful as well to my colleagues and friends at the Center on Human Policy, in the Division of Special Education and Rehabilitation, and in the School of Education at Syracuse University—especially Sari Knopp Biklen, Robert Bogdan, Alison Ford, Luanna Meyer, and Steven Taylor—for their comments on drafts of several chapters; to Peter Knoblock for taking on my administrative responsibilities while I was on leave for a semester; and to Rosemary Alibrandi for her many manuscript corrections and her constant support.

Schooling without Labels

Chapter I

Achieving Regular Lives

ONE PURPOSE OF *Schooling without Labels* is to demonstrate that in some families children with disabilities have become full participants in family life. The experiences especially of six families show the contradiction between what some parents have achieved for their children and what society and its social policies allow. This book attempts to identify the principles of inclusion that govern the lives of these families and might be extended to education and other social institutions. It examines the ways in which educational and social policy and schooling usually resist but could endorse and replicate these parents' vision.

The families interviewed for this book are not representative of all families of children with disabilities. They were selected primarily for two reasons. First, they have all actively sought inclusion of their children in typical schools and in typical community settings: each family has been active in advocacy for inclusive schooling, and each participated in either the Center on Human Policy in Syracuse, New York, or the Integration Action Group and Frontier College in Toronto, Canada. Second, members of several of these families are regarded as having *severe* disabilities, permitting the idea of inclusion to be examined from the broadest perspective.

Family members were interviewed over a year and a half period. The children were observed at home, at school or in other program settings, and in a variety of social situations. The Accetta, Galati, Lehr, Till, and Woronko families wanted their own names used in this book; the names of other interviewees are pseudonyms.

1

One Family's Introduction to the Social Meaning of Disability

Rose Galati first heard the term "mental retardation" applied to her daughter Felicia when a social worker came to her home to interview her. "At about ten months doctors were beginning to give us numbers to call. A social worker came from Surrey Center [for social service and education]," she recalls. "It was 'What's your name?' 'What's your address?' 'When did you realize your daughter was mentally retarded?' and 'What's her birth date?'"

The idea that Felicia could be *retarded* came as a shock to Rose and her husband Dominic, and they certainly had not considered what mental retardation might mean later: having to carry the label "a retarded child" everywhere; separate schools, separate classes, and rejection from the neighborhood school; awkwardness among relatives and friends not sure of what to say or how to respond; and a never ending stream of unsolicited advice. Mental retardation. "Is that what we're talking about?" Rose asked. She hadn't thought about it before; she didn't know specifically what it meant. In retrospect, she recalled hints that neither she nor Dom had picked up on. The doctor had said, for example, "She's not quite holding her bottle yet," and "she's not quite reaching those milestones." But they had talked with the doctor about cerebral palsy, not about an intellectual disability.

After the social worker's visit, Felicia entered an infant stimulation program, the first of several special, disabled-only programs in which she would be placed. From there she went on to a nursery school for students with visual impairments, located in the wing of an elementary school. But in a short while this school rejected her as "not high functioning enough"; as in the so-called able-bodied world, there are ability and status hierarchies within disability groups. The other students in the nursery program were considered intellectually typical or close to it, whereas Felicia was assumed to have a severe disability. Rose Galati remembers feeling as if she and her husband were puppets, directed here and there for services, not knowing really very much about what it all meant or what options might be available. They remember the feeling "We're in other people's hands."

When Felicia was old enough for regular school, the Galatis were living in metropolitan Toronto, which then offered only separate programs, and she attended a disabled-only school. When Rose and Dom settled in a suburb called Mississauga, they were again instructed to place her in a special school, this one a forty-five minute ride each way from their home. With each new placement, the Galatis were being socialized to the world of disability. They were learning that disability meant separate programs, long hours for children on buses, few program options, and dependence on professionals.

Throughout this time, the Surrey Center maintained contact with the Galatis. When Rose became pregnant with a second child, a caseworker suggested placing Felicia in a special home: "They were encouraging us to look for homes because we were going to have a normal child. After all, this [having a child with a disability] wasn't going to happen again. And we should look for a place *just in case* we might need more time for this normal child and *just in case* we couldn't cope with Felicia." The Galatis visited such a home. Shuddering, Rose recalls that when she recognized one little girl there, a staff member told her not to say hello or touch her. The only children out on the playground were those who could "walk, talk, and were toilet trained." The other eleven children were seated in front of a television set that was playing only static.

Rose and Dom were so depressed by the thought of sending Felicia to such a place that they began to question what they were being told. Up to this time, they had accepted the many programs that kept Felicia separate from other children, but they could not warm to this home. Rose remembers family and friends saying, "Well, Rose, no one is saying that Felicia should live here. What we're saying is fill out the papers *just in case*. Fill out the papers because you might not be able to cope. Your normal child is going to need your attention." Rose and Dom knew that "Felicia was being written off. When we left there we swore that never, *neverrrr* would our child darken the door of that place."

As Rose prepared to go into the hospital for the birth of her second child, she asked for a private room. She had come to accept others' attitudes about Felicia—that the child was an imposition on them, if not on herself. "I didn't want to upset other mothers," she reasoned. "I didn't think that at this joyous time it was right to bring all this baggage about my other child and my feelings." If she wasn't prepared to send her daughter away, at least she was willing to keep her out of view. She would participate in society's distancing of people with disabilities. Then, when the new baby was born Rose remembers the family consoling Felicia: "Don't worry, we're going to love you too. You're with us too. We're never going to abandon you. Now you've got a sister who's going to help you and take care of you."

The birth went well, but on the third day, Maria had a seizure. Rose let out a scream. The nurses rushed Maria back to the nursery. They told Rose to "calm down, just calm down." To Rose, this seizure looked precisely like the one that had precipitated Felicia's disability, but the nurses told her they saw nothing. They believed that Rose was just overanxious because of her experience with her other daughter. Pediatricians checked the child but could find nothing wrong. Then, when Maria was a month old, she "seizured" on the pediatrician's examining table. "What's *that*?" Rose exclaimed. She was sure the doctor would say, "It's a seizure." Instead, he told her it was the "rooting reflex" of a child looking for its mother's milk: "Look, I can get her to do it on her other side," he said, rubbing her other cheek. But she did not respond. It took months for doctors to adopt Rose's diagnosis. Maria's stiffening body signaled seizures, and the seizures caused a profound intellectual disability. It is not clear whether an earlier diagnosis could have prevented or reduced the degree of her disabilities.

Caring for two children with disabilities was difficult. Parents on both sides of the family, as well as brothers and sisters, kept telling Rose that the work was too much, that trying to handle the two children herself was unrealistic. They argued, "Place Maria," who is the more disabled of the two children. Although now she finds her relatives helpful with her children, they weren't at the beginning: "Not once did they say, 'Can I baby sit?' or 'Can I make one meal a week?'" So when Maria was just twenty-one months old, she went to live in a modern four-home complex where each home served five children, all of whom had severe physical and intellectual disabilities. It was a far nicer, more personal place than the facility they had investigated for Felicia. A product of the anti-institutions reform movement, it had been established as an alternative to the impersonal, custodial institutions.

While she was there, Maria entered a junior kindergarten for four-year-old children at the regular neighborhood Catholic school. She was the only child in the class who had a disability. One day when Rose visited the class, she had what she later recognized as a momentous interchange.

" Are you Maria's helper?" one of Maria's classmates asked.
" No."
" Are you her friend?" he then asked.
" No, I'm her mother."
" You're her mother? Do you live here?"
" No, I live in Mississauga. Maria lives in a group residence," Rose explained.
" Why don't you live here?" the boy asked, never thinking his question impertinent.
" Good question," Rose thought to herself.

They *were* good questions. Adults wouldn't dream of asking them. After all, she had decided that she couldn't cope. But to these children the idea of living in a special home, away from parents, did not make sense; they wouldn't want that kind of treatment themselves. It troubled Rose that they said as much.

Rose and Dom decided to bring Maria home. The government provided a cash allowance to help offset the extra expenses of raising children with severe disabilities. It had cost the government in excess of $30,000 for Maria's care at the group home; at her family's home it would cost less than half that amount to support both children. But eligibility guidelines required Rose and Dom to say that without a government subsidy, their daughters were in "imminent danger of being institutionalized." On one hand, such a rule was merely one of many that had to be adhered to as part of "being in" the social service system; it would have to be tolerated or finessed. On the other hand, it was a demeaning requirement, typical of many welfare policies and rooted in the traditional ideology of charity. The reasoning is that unless charity rewards only the most desperate cases, and only those that first try to help themselves, it might create a beggar class, dependent on the "easy handout." The Galatis found the eligibility requirement offensive. They did not want to label their children impossible burdens, and after the sense of loss they had felt when Maria was away from them, they were unwilling to consider ever sending either daughter away again. Rose compromised with the bureaucracy's need to justify family support payments: "My daughter will never be institutionalized. Neither . . . will her sister. The only thing is, I can't guarantee to you that you won't have four people to deal with if I don't get help." Those requiring institutionalization, she said sarcastically, would be her husband and herself.

Maria's homecoming marked a dramatic shift in Rose and Dom's perspective on their children. The way they saw it, raising children with disabilities was difficult but rewarding work. Since they required support, if society was reluctant to give that support, they would ask society to change: "People tell me I'm unrealistic. Well it's unrealistic for all of you or any of you to expect that I can survive without my kids. I want my kids. I didn't have children just because it was some sort of accident. I had kids because I wanted to love them and raise them. I need help with that. I can't do it my-self."

When she said she needed "help," Rose Galati did not mean that she and Dom needed special schools or treatment programs of the sort that they had been directed to in the past. Once Rose and Dom became comfortable in their ability to raise Maria and Felicia at home, they wanted other people to become just as accepting. They wanted to have their children in the community, with them when they went shopping, at family gatherings, and in the schools. They wanted regular schools and even regular classes for their children. They wanted them to have friends.

They met resistance almost immediately. Local school officials tried to bar Felicia and Maria from regular classes. That infuriated Rose and Dom: "I'll be damned if the education system is going to work diametrically opposed to me. I can't believe that people would think that it's okay to say to a parent, 'I'm sorry, but the system isn't ready for you.'" When the Galatis appealed to the superintendent, he allowed the girls to enroll, but the struggle was not over. Rose remembers that the principal waited until the end of the year to declare, "It didn't work. Our professionals [teachers and psychologists] say it didn't work." Rose and Dom believe that the principal wanted to make it look as if the school had tried integration, even though he had always intended to prove that it couldn't work. Rose told him so:

I didn't want to accept their purposeful failures. I could accept that a teacher didn't know what to do because he or she didn't have the right kind of support or people or whatever, but that's different. I said, "I think you people had this planned all along. I don't think you want Felicia and Maria here. And you know as well as I that this is the meeting where you say, "Look Dom and Rose, we tried our very best and we were really good and now we want you to be good and take them away." But what I was thinking was that what my children needed—the staff, including an aide for each daughter—could be provided right in the classroom.

Rumors circulated that the principal was at odds with the school district over the integration issue. The Galatis heard from one source inside the district that the principal had threatened to leave if the girls stayed. Some people expected Rose and Dom to cave in under all the pressure, but they did not. "If this man has such a big problem with my kids," Rose told a small group of supporters, "then I support him in his decision to leave the school. He should go." She was motivated not only by the injustice that school exclusion posed but also by her belief that school was essential to her daughters' welfare: "My kids need that school. I know that my kids need that school. We live here."

Many parents in Canada, the United States, Australia, England, and other countries have sought and achieved integration of their children with disabilities in regular schools. But in most instances, parents have had to negotiate with school officials. As shown in later chapters, educational professionals usually organize the education of students with disabilities into more or less restrictive (that is, segregated) programs, ranging from institutional or special school placements to separate treatment within the regular class. Researchers have typically framed the issue of school integration as a debate over "best methods": In other words, how much integration makes sense for which children, with which disabilities? To such professionals, integration is an educational method that might or might not be beneficial, depending on the student.

Rose Galati framed her argument for Felicia and Maria differently. What she wanted from the school was what she and Dom provided for their daughters at home—the chance to participate in everyday life. They had come to accept and feel happy about their daughters. They were buoyed by reports of progress: For example, that Felicia could now walk into her classroom and find her desk— "Don't you know what a big step that is for Felicia?" Rose asks rhetorically—or that other students were helping Maria with her meals and talking to her, even if she could only make a sound in response. What they found problematic was the fact that many segments of the world outside the family seemed to have difficulty seeing Maria and Felicia as ordinary people. They believe that too many people regard the girls as extra burdens on the schools, as "different" children who should be sent to special centers and homes, and as reasons for parental despair. Rose rejects that view: "I always say it's not hard to be the parents of my children; it's hard to go out the door and to tell people that it is all right to be the parents of my children." She worries that as long as people believe she and Dom cannot be happy with Felicia and Maria close at hand, the girls will not find a place in the everyday world.

It is often the case that certain incidents symbolize larger struggles. A four-year-old's questions sparked a new beginning for Rose and her children, and within a very short while Rose was asking society the same kind of question: Why can't Felicia and Maria attend school in the neighborhood where their parents live? Embedded in the stories of other parents too (e.g., see Featherstone 1981; and Massie and Massie 1976) and those of people with disabilities are similarly transforming events, seemingly modest incidents of much larger import than their face value would suggest. Judith Snow, a Canadian disability rights activist, recently reminisced about how people tend to see you when you live the life of a special child. Like Rose Galati, Snow (1988, 146–47) recollects a seemingly ordinary event:

> Once a year some group would put on a party and invite all the disabled children and their parents. This would always include a turkey dinner or hot dogs and ice cream, and each child would always get a present. At other times these same people would raise money to buy equipment or send us off to the camp for "crippled" children. I sometimes wonder if those men hated the parties as much as we did, especially after we got to be ten years old or so. Our parents wanted us to go because they depended on their charity to meet our extraordinary needs, but we always knew that these people were not a real part of our lives, and that they didn't really want to know us as friends. Otherwise I could have gone to camp with their sons and daughters and I could have visited some of them at their homes, and they would have visited mine. As it was, we never got to see each other as real people, nor did they ever get to see me as real.

The professional literature characterizes the vision of people like Rose Galati and Judith Snow in terms such as "normalization" (enabling people to participate in typical routines and activities of daily life), "acceptance" (Bogdan and Taylor 1987), "complete schooling" (Biklen 1985), "Circles of Friends" (Forest 1987; Perske 1988), and "community integration" (Taylor, Biklen, and Knoll 1987). Judith Snow and Rose and Dom Galati think of it simply as leading regular lives, in common with other people.

Is the Concept of "Special" Inevitable?

Being your own person is the first prerequisite of inclusion, but that comes with difficulty for people who have been branded disabled. The case records of students classified as disabled bespeak deficits: "moderately retarded student unable to communicate in complex sentences"; "not capable of fully independent living without support"; "has difficulty making friends"; "age 15, reading on

grade 2 level"; "poor impulse control, student requires close supervision and management." Such records are littered with deficit labels and statements that sound more like conclusions than
prognoses. Yet Judith Snow and the Galatis do not think in these
deficit terms. Indeed, they are not comfortable at all with the concept of disability.

Questions then arise: Are Felicia and Maria Galati handicapped?
Judith Snow can move only one thumb, but is it helpful to call her
handicapped? People who have been classified as disabled often reject "handicapped" and other disability labels altogether. When
they speak of disability in referring to themselves, they do so in a
way that rejects traditional societal definitions, those that involve
deficit counting or that speak of *the* handicapped or *the* retarded—
terms that make some disability the all-defining characteristic of the
person. Nancy Kaye (1981, 56), for example, notes that the word
"handicapped" was never used in her home when she was growing
up, even though she has spina bifida. She knew that she was different, but she did not feel less valuable as a person. It was not until
she was out in the world that she encountered "lots of messages
about being handicapped." Similarly, Paul Hunt (quoted in Shearer
1981, 21) writes of the contradiction between the social value or
status associated with wealth or with family position (parent, husband, wife) and the reality that even though some people with disabilities do not acquire such status, they nevertheless "retain an
ineradicable conviction that they are still fully human in all that is
ultimately necessary."

People with disabilities reject everyday labels that lower their
status to that of a dependent, hopeless group. In her interviews
with forty-five women, all identified by society as disabled,
Gwyneth Ferguson Mathews discovered a host of words that they
found offensive. "I don't like 'patient,'" one woman explains; the
term makes her think of someone who is sick, as in a hospital, and
she does not consider herself that. A "patient" is one who waits for
the action of others; it implies passivity. She also objects to the
term "case": "Let's see—there's a case of pop, and a case of measles,
and lawyers take cases. But I don't like being one." To be a case
means to become an object that others can treat; it makes a patho-

logical equation between the disability and the whole person. Similarly, Mathews and her respondents object to "suffering," which connotes pity; "victim," which connotes powerlessness and dehumanization; and "crippled," which they say derived (before the advent of wheelchairs) from the verb "to creep" and conjures up images of a beggar class (Mathews 1983, 126–34).

In stark contrast, Nancy Mairs adopts "crippled" as her label of preference, with the intent to shock: "People—crippled or not—wince at the word 'cripple,' as they do not at 'handicapped' or 'disabled.' Perhaps I want them to wince. I want them to see me as a tough customer, one to whom the fates/gods/viruses have not been kind, but who can face the brutal truth of her existence squarely. As a cripple, I swagger." She selects "cripple" as a way of saying, "I accept myself for who I am, and I am going to force you to accept me on the same terms." Though she chooses the term for herself, however, in a kind of tough defiance of her condition and of society's discomfort with it and with her, she would not impose it on anyone else (Mairs 1986, 9–10).

People labeled "retarded" have also rejected disability labels. Like Gwyneth Ferguson Mathews and her forty-five respondents, they ask why they can't be called by their names. It is no accident that people who had been labeled retarded formed a self-advocacy group called "People First." Similarly, they led a successful campaign in Canada to change the name of their sponsoring organization from the Canadian Association for the Mentally Retarded to the Canadian Association for Community Living. Patrick Worth, president of the Ontario chapter of People First, was a leading proponent of the name change. "Nobody has the right to label someone 'retarded,'" he says; the label is a kind of punishment that stops people from getting jobs and prohibits them from living in the community. "It is demoralizing to see someone as a label instead of [as] somebody," he writes. "I am a somebody. My name is Patrick Worth. I am not retarded. I don't think anyone is. I think labels are unnecessary" (Worth 1988, 48). Others apparently agree. Sociologist Robert Bogdan concludes that people labeled retarded say "I'm not retarded" not because they can achieve high scores on intelligence or other tests but because they "have never really thought of

. . . [themselves] as bad" (Bogdan 1980, 78). In other words, they understand that in the cultural trade of labels, the term "retarded" brings negative value. In everyday parlance it is a pejorative as well as a psychological term.

If we can agree that such labels are not helpful, does that mean that Felicia and Maria Galati do not have educational needs that are different from those of other students? It is both trite and unhelpful to answer this question with the glib declaration that "all children have special needs." Of course all people are different in subtle ways, but some people are *quite* different. Maria and Felicia do need different or drastically modified school curricula. Maria can be spoken to, but she does not respond with words. Felicia can be taught to recognize some symbols, but she has not yet been able to show whether or not she can recognize letters or read. She can give only one sign: tapping her leg to indicate that she wants to go to the bathroom. She needs the assistance of another person to cup her hands over a plate when setting the table, although she is becoming more self-sufficient in this task. So there can really be no debate that both children need significant support to live in the community.

The issue, then, is what form that support should take and what we are to call it. Should it be considered special or unusual? Should it be offered in segregated locations such as disabled-only transit service, special classes, and special schools? Should we talk about the services, whatever they are, in a language that connotes difference: special education, invalid transport, handicapped housing, sheltered workshops, adult day care? Should we go one step further with the nomenclature and impose images of pity, hopelessness, and despair? Wolfensberger (1978) has chronicled examples of such language in his sarcastic essay "The Ideal Human Service for a Societally Devalued Group": a transit service called "Tender Loving Care"; St. Jude's Hospital, named for the patron saint of hopeless causes, as a center for children with disabilities; and Hope Haven, a private institution for people considered disabled.

Of course, disabilities do not naturally evoke forced segregation and ignominious or euphemistic labels. Particular societies create such a fate. Lewis Anthony Dexter sees society's treatment of mental retardation as arbitrary, problem-creating, and self-perpetuating but presumably changeable. He asks us to imagine a society in which clumsy people are considered a major social problem. The disability would be gawkiness. In a society that valued grace, designers would fashion machines that required graceful operators. Industry would hire people on the basis of grace, not because grace was essential to business activity but because grace itself was prized. Schools would test for levels of gracefulness. "And in many cases, parents and schools would be so embarrassed and bothered by the presence of gawky children that they would send them to special custodial institutions where they would not be a constant reminder of parental or pedagogical inadequacy" (Dexter 1962, 223). Dexter developed his analogy to question societal treatment of people it considered slow, possibly mildly retarded, but the analogy holds for people with severe disabilities as well. Maria and Felicia Galati were each prohibited from attending regular classes with their non-disabled peers. Although officials excluded them on the grounds that they could not benefit from those classes as then constituted, it is not impossible to imagine that the classes could have been adapted to grant them access.

Similarly, there is nothing in the nature of human existence which dictates that people shall be valued in accordance with their intellectual abilities. Such standards are socially created: "A society which increasingly focuses on 'excellence,' meaning thereby intellectual excellence, as does ours, tends more and more to discriminate against stupidity" (Dexter 1962, 225). Although we may feel uncomfortable with Dexter's free use of the term "stupidity," he probably intended it (much as Mairs chooses "cripple" over softer terms like "special") to emphasize that any negative label, even if partially masked, harms those to whom it is applied. In a footnote, he hypothesizes that people labeled "stupid" would probably benefit from living in a society "that attached more weight to *moral* excellence"—by which, presumably, he means helpfulness, concern, and mutual interdependence.

This discussion leads us back to my central theme: Can schools and other social institutions adopt the vision of those families in which the person with a disability is a full participant in everyday life? How would society have to alter its values, its notion of excellence, its evaluation of individuals, its language, its forms of mutual support, and other factors? What would its philosophy of education be? If some families have achieved this hoped-for inclusion to a greater extent than have other social institutions, it follows that we should look first to these families for guidance. What do their experiences tell us about the social changes necessary to enable people with disabilities to participate in schools and other aspects of everyday life?

Family Lessons: A Framework for Schools

The literature on families and children with disabilities does not always reveal harmonious, integrated social units. Nevertheless, there is substantial evidence that *many* families do achieve what might be described as full inclusion of children with even the most severe disabilities. In the assumptions and actions of the Galatis we can observe ideas and practices that begin to explain the inclusion and how it might translate to schools.

Recognizing That People without Special Training Can Raise Children with Disabilities

Parents whose child has a disability rarely start out with expertise in managing disability or in special child-rearing techniques. True, they may often (but don't always) benefit from consultation with an array of experts, yet in the final analysis the parents themselves, lay people, often achieve remarkable success in raising their children. For example, Rose and Dom Galati learned the proper way of helping Maria to eat. They taught Felicia to walk up and down stairs. The analogue in schools would be that with proper consultation and support, regular educators could achieve a similar ability to educate students, whatever their disabilities.

Avoiding Labels

Parents do not generally refer to their children by disability labels. They know and appreciate them by their names, by their interests, by their habits, and by their abilities. The Galatis reject disability labels as unhelpful. We could imagine schools approaching students from a similarly noncategorical, nonlabeling perspective. There would be no more ED (emotionally disturbed), LD (learning disabled), MR (mentally retarded), BD (behavior disordered), NI (neurologically impaired), or otherwise "special" students. "The handicapped" would cease to exist as a concept.

Making Inclusion Unconditional

Obviously, parents do not impose intelligence tests or other exams to establish the eligibility of children to participate in family life; it would be bizarre if they did. Rather, the Galatis and many other families promote their children, looking for ways for them to participate in mainstream activities. The question for schools, as for families, is this: Should they fashion themselves as gatekeepers, engaged in a careful if somewhat arbitrary sorting process, "putting children in their place"? Or is it the role of schools to be gate openers, creating opportunities? Like families, schools could use the crucible of everyday events as the proper context for assessing how to include and educate students; this would be an alternative to the common practice of assessing-to-place. The latter tends to catalogue students' deficits or disabilities. The former focuses only on issues of teaching and learning.

Accepting Diversity

Like the Galatis, many families are shocked when they first discover that they have a child with a disability. Some are traumatized both by the sudden recognition that their child is not what they had imagined and by his or her actual appearance or ability. But families' perceptions change. Subsequent chapters describe children who initially seemed very different from other children yet whose families have come not only to understand and accept their appearance and behavior, to the point of seeing them as ordinary, but in fact to appreciate these children. In the late nineteenth and early twentieth centuries there were states and provinces and school districts in the United States and Canada that systematically segregated students with disabilities in order to hide them from public view; they were considered abhorrent. Schools have a choice: to perpetuate the disabled-as-unsightly-freak perspective or, as many families have done, to transform their notions of who is acceptable.

Identifying Individual Gifts

Not only do families come to recognize their children as "acceptable"; they also come to love, appreciate, and admire them. In her writing and speeches Judith Snow asserts that every child has "gifts." Two of the children described in the next chapter have histories of abusing themselves, yet their families discover reasons for admiring them. Interestingly, the manner in which this happens and the particular qualities or "gifts" that the parents uncover are intimately connected to how the children learn, how they communicate, and how their teachers—including their parents—must interact with them.

Maintaining Equal Status

When Rose Galati describes her discomfort at the advice of others to "place" Felicia, in anticipation of her giving birth to a "normal" child, we cannot help being aware that she did not want to think of the two children as unequal. Indeed, she has come to see Felicia and Maria as the equals not only of each other but of her nondisabled niece and of all other children. Applied to schools, this concept suggests that irrespective of ability levels, students are truly peers, and that therefore the education of the student with the most severe intellectual disability or multiple disabilities is as important as the education of students who have no disabilities.

Providing Constant Inclusion

One of the hallmarks of raising children is that they are *constantly* present. In inclusive families, children with disabilities participate in literally every aspect of family life. Felicia and Maria Galati, for example, attend family events such as weddings; they go on holidays with their parents to Florida and elsewhere; they go to ball games; they go shopping; and they "hang out" in the neighborhood with other children. Every night, with the help of an adult, Felicia Galati sets the dinner table. Similarly, she helps to fold and put away her own clothes. Families often develop accommodations to make such participation possible. The fact that a child cannot be taught to swim, for example (physical disabilities may prevent it) does not mean that the child cannot go to the beach, go into the water, play in the sand. In schools, the issue of how to make activities available to the child with a disability runs counter to many of the ways in which schools are currently structured.

Considering the Future

The parents who take their children with disabilities to preschool programs are already concerned about what will become of them in future years. They may believe that the preschool program will give them social contact with other children, but they also hope that it will begin preparing them for school. Typically, parents of preschoolers are already concerned about what kind of education their children will receive when they reach school age. Some families even begin at this early age to worry about what will become of the children when they graduate from public school. Will they be able to live independently? Will they be capable of working? Will people accept them? Such concerns motivated the Galatis to find Felicia a job with a local hairdresser. Similarly, schools might ask, "Is anyone worried that these students are missing opportunities, are falling behind, or are receiving unproductive educational programs?" Where are the school reform reports that express a sense of national outrage for the inferior, unnecessarily segregated education of students with severe and multiple disabilities? Parents' worries bespeak a sense of urgency, sometimes mistaken for unreasonableness.

Building Relationships

The fact that the Galatis' home is often filled with neighborhood children or that Felicia and Maria are invited to play at a neighbor's home is no accident. Rose works at including other children in their family activities, and that has given neighborhood children opportunities to get to know Felicia and Maria and to become comfortable with them. This effort to help her children find acceptance is not unusual, although it may be more deliberate and determined than that of many other parents. Parents of children with disabilities understand that their children's future depends significantly on the kind of relationships they will have and on their ability to have friends. Consequently, they are puzzled and often annoyed at the suggestion that "socialization" is unrelated to the core of school curricula and the purpose of schooling. The tension for schools in addressing this agenda is not unlike the dilemma that parents face—how to create opportunities and increase the ability of students to relate to one another without making the situation artificial and therefore alienating.

Seeking Adequate Resources

Parents frequently complain that they must "make a case" for assistance in such matters as accessibility alterations to their homes, child-care expenses, reimbursement of expenditures for such equipment as wheelchair inserts and communication systems, respite services, homemaker services, accessible transportation, and medical bills. For Rose Galati, "making a case" for funding is little different from the nineteenth-century requirement that charity recipients sing for their supper. What the Galatis want, of course, is for support to become a natural part of the social fabric, available on demand without the requirement of begging or submitting to a means test or filing an affidavit of extraordinary need. This becomes an issue in schools wherever children's right-of-access is held hostage to the provision of special government funding.

Sharing Stories

The stories in this book are not unlike the stories that parents of children with disabilities share with one another and with people they believe are supportive of their children's progress. A child's election to the school's student council, a child's sudden advance from knowing only four or five words to knowing five hundred, and a child's newly formed friendship—these are the contents of such stories. Parents tell them as evidence that their faith in their children's potential is justified. The stories also mark progress, justifying optimism for the children's future. In this sense, parents study their children, looking for any small indication of growth or interest, something on which change and development can be built. The fact that parents tell such stories reveals the seriousness with which they regard their children. If schools were to imitate such storytelling, principals and teachers would know and talk about evidence of learning by even the most severely disabled student. The fact that similar stories or accounts have not ordinarily been part of the typical principal's conversations about school life is probably indicative of the marginal status that students with disabilities have held in schools.

The central question raised in the next chapter is whether the concept of inclusion can apply to *all* children, *all* families, and, by extension, to *all* schools.

CHAPTER II

The Inclusion Philosophy

PARENTS OFTEN talk differently about their children than other people do. This is especially true for parents of children with disabilities. It is certainly true of parents who advocate radical changes in the ways schools and other parts of society treat their children. These parents have a vision for their children that may be at odds with society's vision. Are the parents "unrealistic," as some professionals would say? Are they more hopeful than circumstances and their children's abilities warrant? Is disappointment inevitable? Deep down, do these parents really believe that the vision of their children participating in the everyday world can come true? Are they destined to be disappointed?

The three families described in this chapter are determined, combative, and resilient. Their philosophies of child rearing and of education are reminiscent of Sylvia Ashton-Warner's (1963) and Paulo Freire's (1970) approaches to literacy. The children, their actions, and—to the extent they are discernible—their feelings, their thoughts, and their world are the *text*. Like Freire and Ashton-Warner with their students, the parents look to their children for communication of intent and interest; they believe that their children's best learning will occur as part of a natural desire to participate in family life, in school, and in the community. They define good education as interactive education. Not surprisingly, the parents want schools to share this perspective.

A Child's Signs of Wanting Inclusion

Mary Lou Accetta adopted her son Melvin. At the age of five he had been removed from his birth parents' home because of suspected neglect and physical abuse. The local social services department placed him in a retardation institution in Syracuse, N.Y., for a weekend and, over the next two weeks, in five different foster homes. Each foster family in turn returned him to the institution, complaining of his difficult behavior, which included climbing on the roof at three o'clock in the morning, or turning on the stove and putting his hand over the flame (which was one of the ways he is alleged to have been abused), or starting fires. A temporary three-and-a-half-month placement back at the institution stretched into two and a half years. Because he could not speak effectively, Melvin's language communication was limited to five manual signs meaning eat, run, more, music, and help. The unit where he lived had no other children who could speak, nor were there any children his age; the next youngest was twelve. Only two residents besides Melvin were able to walk; everyone else used a wheelchair.

Mary Lou met Melvin at Jowonio, an early childhood and kindergarten school where she worked. His classroom had fifteen children, ten nondisabled and five with disabilities. At that time, she recalls, "he always needed to have an adult right next to him because he would pull hair or kick people or bite other kids as well as teachers." Also, he was a "runner"—institutional language for anyone who ran away from the institution. Melvin often ran away from the school and from Mary Lou as well. She took that as a cue that he was aware. When he was still only five years old, he left his unit at the institution, went down to the ground level on the elevator, got past the receptionist at the main desk and out the door. An hour later the receptionist took a call from the local McDonald's, two blocks away but across two busy streets. "There is a little boy here demanding a hamburger and I think he is one of the kids that has come down here with your folks," the caller announced. When the institution staff went to retrieve him, they found him making the sign for "eat." Obviously he knew where he was going. He knew what he wanted.

Not everyone shared Mary Lou's positive assessment of Melvin. She recalls an incident when he was nearly eight, after he had been living with her for four months. She had taken him to church with her. The service was signed, so Melvin was paying attention: within three months of his moving in with her, he had learned two hundred signs; he had begun with only five. One of the administrators from his former unit at the institution was seated three rows behind them. After the service he approached Mary Lou and said in all seriousness, "I want you to know I am still keeping his bed open [human service professionals often refer to residential placements as 'beds']; he'll be back." Mary Lou couldn't believe her ears. "Excuse me?" she said. "He's not going to make it," the man continued, "and I just want you to know it's all right to send him back." Mary Lou still feels angry about such attitudes toward Melvin, even though she knows they were probably widely shared. Having seen so much evidence that this boy knew what he wanted and of his ability to express himself, she was bewildered as much as furious that other people couldn't or wouldn't see what she saw.

Every story she tells about Melvin is a report of his growth. One time he ran away from a new sitter. After frantically searching for him and even asking the police to help, Mary Lou discovered him sitting naked in a stream. He explained to her that he had climbed some trees in the cemetery, then had crossed the busy street and come to the stream, which he had visited with a previous sitter. She asked him how he had expected to get home, and he showed her the streets he'd planned to take. Despite the severe fright she had experienced, Mary Lou could not help marveling at Melvin's seeming ease with himself and the community. He knew what he wanted and what he was doing, even if he could not communicate easily with the people around him.

When he first came to the Jowonio school, Melvin was not toilet trained, and "bathroom" was not one of his signs. Beyond the five signs he knew, he did not appear to be learning more and seemed unresponsive to pictures. There was reason to believe that he would not communicate. His typical way of getting something was to grab it or stamp his feet and yell until the people around him could guess what he wanted and give it to him. Mary Lou worked on his communication. When he displayed his "behaviors," Mary Lou and the Jowonio teachers would hold up what he wanted, such as a carton of milk, then show him the sign for milk and say, "You need to tell me milk." If he produced anything even close to the sign for what he wanted, he was given the item and a lot of praise: "We did a lot of just telling him how good that was and wasn't it exciting that he was talking, really making a big fuss about it." Mary Lou and her housemate signed nearly everything they said, even signing to each other when they wanted something. Melvin became an incidental observer and soon began his rush to accumulate signs—two hundred in three months.

Melvin's growth during this time was more complex than might be accounted for by a tabulation of his new signs. All through his early days with Mary Lou, he needed assurances: guarantees that he wouldn't be returned to the institution, evidence that there was enough food in the house, proof that he was loved. Mary Lou recalls his "wonderful stories about when he used to live at the institution." The stories are not really wonderful at all; they are frightening, but she thinks of them as wonderful because he can tell them, because he can express his feelings about his life. He calls the institution "the big house" and tells of how big people at the big house used to steal his food. For the first six months with Mary Lou, Melvin hid food under his mattress and pillow each night. He would slip food under his shirt and sneak it up to his room, a skill he undoubtedly learned at the institution. Once he realized there seemed to be no limit to the food available to him, he went from hiding it to opening the kitchen cabinets to verify that the food was still there. If Mary Lou ran out of some item, such as milk, Melvin would become hysterical for nearly an hour.

Several months later, after food was less of a concern for him, Melvin explained to Mary Lou that he was surprised food came from a store. "If you asked him where people get food," she recalls, "he would tell you it comes up on the elevator. It comes on a cart." That was his "experience" at the institution. He was fascinated that you could go to the store and bring home food. The second week he was with Mary Lou, they went to the store, bought groceries, and came home to cook them. He stood in the kitchen helping to break one egg after another. He signed "cook," seemingly amazed at the process of preparing food.

Mary Lou Accetta was determined that her vision for Melvin would come true. He had been labeled severely retarded, severely behavior-disordered, hyperactive, and epileptic. Yet she saw ability and promise: "I always had the sense that there was a bright little kid under there. He was reacting so strongly to his environment." Before she adopted Melvin, she would bring him home for weekends. As she drove him back to the institution, he would suddenly jump down on the floor of the car, banging his head and laughing hysterically. Mary Lou would literally have to drag him through the corridors to his unit. If she told him to behave differently, he only became wilder. But when she finally said to him, "You're right; you shouldn't be here," he stopped and listened. He demanded to be taken seriously. Even though he could not speak, he demanded to be heard. And although one interpretation of his behavior was that he was being outrageous, another suggests that he was communicating in the only way he knew how—by screaming, kicking, and trying to run away.

During Melvin's first Christmas with Mary Lou, when they were at her relatives' house, Melvin picked up a big glass vase and smashed it. Presumably he did it to show that he was angry or perhaps anxious. Mary Lou remembers her relatives' looks of horror when she said, "Good boy. You're really mad but you didn't hurt anybody."

At age eleven, Melvin's surroundings still played a large part in his life. He seemed to feel secure. He had a home. He would literally run *to* school. And he liked being with other students who talked and played and interacted with him. At this point he was attempting to speak, and his words could be understood about 50 percent of the time, especially by people who knew him. He wouldn't use signs unless people just could not understand his speech. He referred to himself as being and acting "like the other kids."

It's not as if Melvin suddenly became a different person. He is the same person, but his life circumstances have changed. He still has tantrums and outbursts that Mary Lou admits cause her discomfort: "Having been a special ed teacher, I was sort of surprised at my own reaction. But it is real different all of a sudden when it is your kid doing the obnoxious behavior." She and Mel are well known at the local grocery store. Once, when she had to tell him he could not have every kind of cereal but just two, he smashed a big container of sauce on the floor, splashing it on a woman who was walking by. The woman responded angrily: "Isn't this boy big enough to know better?" Reflecting on that incident, remembering that she had not expected to be so uncomfortable, Mary Lou reminds herself that she needs to focus on what Melvin may be experiencing and not so much on her own feelings.

Melvin has difficulty with "first times." If he is entering a new situation, either he's not fully comfortable with it or he wants to test Mary Lou's limits. She says she has learned just to weather the first time of anything, knowing that the next times will be easier, whether it is visiting a friend's house or ice skating. Melvin does not like to be told "no," so if he becomes destructive or grabs at things she does not want him to have, it's virtually disastrous to remonstrate or refuse directly. Mary Lou sets limits in other terms than "no." In the case of destruction, she generalizes: "It's not all right to hurt people, and this is not ours to destroy. I cannot do that. Neither can you. No one can." Similarly, rather than saying, "No, you can't have another cookie" when Melvin grabs for one, she'll likely say, "You can have another cookie tomorrow." Of course, that may work, but it may not, in which case Melvin is likely to pick up the nearest thing and throw it, showing his anger. "If he is really, really upset," says Mary Lou, "he might smack his head against the floor."

Sometimes his angry outbursts seem to be directed at his past as much as at an immediate occurrence. For quite a while, for instance, Melvin would become furious at lunch time, screaming, running around, and throwing things. Mary Lou did not have a clue as to what set him off. Was it something about sitting down for lunch? Wasn't he hungry? Did he want to do something else? Didn't he like the particular food? Usually he would start crying

and then say "no." Finally, Mary Lou realized that each time he saw
a little can of pudding, he would get upset, all the time saying "no,
no." Actually, he loves pudding, but the little cans of pudding reminded him of the institution, where the staff used them as a "rein-
forcer" whenever he did something they considered right.

The institution maintains a large presence in Mel's mind. When
he and Mary Lou were waiting for a doctor's appointment, a staff
resident from the institution came into the waiting room and remarked aloud, "Isn't that Melvin Haynes? Oh boy, I knew him
when he lived at the institution. What a hellion. I could tell you
some stories that would curl your hair." Mary Lou tried to cut him
off, saying, "We really don't want to hear that, thank you," but
Melvin was already up on the couch, diving over the furniture and
breaking a lamp. As everybody in the office turned to look, the
man from the institution said, "See, I told you; that's the kid I
know." All the time Mary Lou was thinking, "That's not the kid I
know"—but would anyone believe her?

He may have been abused at the institution. For months after
coming to live with Mary Lou, Mel slept under his bed instead of
on it. Each time Mary Lou put him back in his bed, he would say
"no" and get back under it. Of course, there was a story behind this
behavior, just as there was a story for the pudding and for his
hoarding of food. One day, Melvin explained that "big people at
the big house" used to crawl into his bed and scare him at night. If
he slept under his bed they couldn't find him.

The public and maybe even some teachers see Mary Lou as putting up with a lot and show surprise that Mel still lives with Mary
Lou. They may marvel at her progress with him, noting that he
now walks to school on his own, but they likely also wonder, "how
she does it. I don't think I could do it." If they see her frantically
hunting for Melvin when he's lost, or sprinting to catch him when
he runs off without warning while walking with her in a mall, or
trying to survive his first time skating or the Christmas visit with
in-laws, they may think, "That's Melvin." Yet her world with
Melvin is more complex than that. He is much more of a person
than just someone who runs, cries, grabs food, or smashes a vase.

Mary Lou Accetta refuses to think about her life with Melvin in *simple* behavioral terms. She knows that if he runs or grabs, she must respond; as the behaviorists would say, there must be consequences. *But* she wants to frame her questions about Melvin's behavior and his life more broadly. What is his world like? How has life treated him? What do people expect of him and how do they show it? How does she herself behave toward Melvin? "If I get to the point where I am dealing with consequences (grabbing, running, throwing something), then chances are I have done something wrong," she says. Mary Lou searches for reasonable ways to channel Melvin's anger and anxiety, like taking him to a track to run if he's feeling a need to run. Above all, she looks to prevent his outbursts by anticipating situations that he'll find difficult and helping him to reinterpret them.

Three years ago, Melvin's class, a public school class of students both with and without disabilities, was preparing to take "levels" tests. Since Melvin was doing prereading exercises—constructing sentences from pictures, for example, rather than reading words, sentences, paragraphs, and books—the teacher did not have a levels test for him. Melvin apparently realized that he might not be involved in the testing. He became upset and started to run around the room, laughing and throwing things. Only after the teacher secured a prereading levels test from another teacher and included Melvin in the testing did he calm down. He worked quietly on the test for an hour and a half, all the time saying to himself, "same as the kids, same as the kids." Mary Lou recalled that the previous year Melvin and an aide had spent the entire day apart from his regular class while the other students took the levels tests. Neither she nor the teachers had known what Melvin had felt about it then, but now he was showing them. Like other incidents with Melvin, this one confirmed her belief that he understood what was happening around him; that somewhere in his background he had learned to cry, throw things, and run in order to get his way; that he could change his behavior; and that if the world around him could anticipate his response to certain situations, then the world could change so that his experience would be different.

By taking Melvin out of the institution, Mary Lou had eradicated the biggest problem in his life. One incident made her certain of that:

> He was sitting on the couch quietly with a book open, just crying. I couldn't imagine what was happening. He had never had quiet moments like that at that point or at least very rarely. I just looked and didn't say anything. He was looking at Burt Blatt's book, *Christmas in Purgatory* [1966, an exposé of abuse in mental retardation institutions]. He looked up and said "big house." It was like he recognized that this was about where he had been. I sat down and we went through the book together. He just cried. At this point he had very little language. It was just amazing to me. . . . He has shown me time and time again, "Don't underestimate me and don't judge me by your outside perceptions."

The point is self-evident: To understand Melvin you have to understand his history, how he thinks about it, and how he relates what is happening in his life now to that history.

Obviously, not everyone agrees with Mary Lou's perspective that education requires a careful combination of inquiry, interpretation, and trial and error. For instance, she was saddened when she visited the "behavioral unit" of a disabled-students-only school, several weeks before our interview, and observed a boy in restraints. In her words, there was "nothing positive happening in the classroom." She found the staff simply

> reacting to negative behavior. It was very controlling but no positive program going on. Maybe they were teaching the child that every time he hit someone, a great big guy would tackle him down to the floor. If you hit, you get tackled, and maybe after a while the kid will decide it is not worth it and stop hitting. But they were not teaching the kid anything about what you do when you are bored with what you are doing, or when you want something, how to ask for it.

Mary Lou wondered what they would do to her son. She imagined the outrage with which he would react to the "behavioral unit" and his frustration: "My kid would spend his whole day on the floor. He is a very strong little boy and I say that with respect; that is why he survives. In a place like this, they would either break his spirit or break his body."

The very quality that such a program would destroy is what gives Mary Lou hope for Mel. He is not just a wild child, as the institution staff had implied. He has ideas, interests, and intent. True, he sometimes acts out his desires and frustrations in difficult ways, but such acts as crying, running, and throwing are really just part of his demanding a future for himself. One day, Mary Lou chanced to observe Melvin nearly mesmerized as he watched a musical performance in his classroom. On the strength of that observation, she dared to take him to a concert of the Syracuse Symphony Orchestra. He sat quietly through a three-hour performance.

It would be mistaken and self-defeating to assume that Melvin can be helped by a regimen of treatment that ignores his everyday experiences and his institutional and other past history, but neither can he be helped by a regimen that is incompatible with his own vision of what he deserves as a person. Mel forces us to question whether society can and will adapt to people who need significant help in finding a way to communicate or to move around in the community. We must ask whether teachers can reasonably be expected to figure out that Melvin may feel excluded if he is not permitted to take a levels test, or whether school districts ought to be asked to transport all students on common buses or teach them how to use the public transit. Will school districts create "regular" classes that include both students like Melvin and those without disabilities? Can others learn to ponder Melvin's occasionally extreme behavior and engage him about its meaning?

Judging from how they act and talk about their experiences, Mary Lou Accetta, Rose Galati, and Judith Snow are of a single mind in believing that such acceptance *is* a reasonable expectation. While they may individually wonder whether their vision will prevail in society, their actions and comments imply an unfaltering allegiance to that vision. For every instance of an outsider's bewilderment about a child's behavior, the parents seem to have a way of interpreting it. For each episode or act of insensitivity to their child or to disability in general, the families seem to have an apt response. Just when the vision appears to fail, the parents offer concrete steps for making it come alive.

Is Inclusion Possible for Everyone?

For Felicia, Maria, and Melvin, inclusion in ordinary life at home and in society has required significant support, and we must question whether the extent of the needed support renders the goal harder to justify or less likely to be achieved. To explore the issue of possible limits to a policy of inclusion, we look next at a family that includes a child who has a history of self-abuse, and then a family that is poor and African American and includes a son with multiple disabilities.

Sue and Bob Lehr are the parents of three children—two girls and a boy—two of whom are adopted. At the time of their son's adoption, when he was only a few months old, neither they nor the adoption agency knew that he had a disability; when it was discovered, the social services department offered to take Ben back. To the Lehrs, this suggestion was unthinkable: "You don't give your child away."

Life with Ben has been rich, if eventful. "Given the opportunity, he will smash his head, he will pull his hair out, he will bite himself, he will cut himself. Given the opportunity, he loves to take a knife and draw straight lines on himself until he bleeds. He has the potential to be as self-abusive as the kids I have seen on the 'tapes'" (that is, television reporting about denying children food, imposing electric shock, forcing them to stand naked, or spraying them with ammonia when they abuse themselves). But the difference, Sue explains, is that they try not to give him the opportunity but to create positive experiences instead, literally replacing his acts of hurting himself with other activities. Nevertheless, a week before my most recent interview with his parents, at the age of fifteen Ben bashed his head into four different windows at home and broke them. Fortunately, he was not badly cut.

Explaining that Ben had been sick and out of school for nearly a week before the incident, Sue Lehr interprets Ben's window smashing either as frustration at not being able to communicate how bad he was feeling or simply as the result of feeling sick. For the family members, communicating with Ben is always a bit like playing Twenty Questions, with Ben making up the rules of the game but not sharing them:

> I know that if he says to me, "I'm sick," that means he is going to vomit. But if he has a cold or runny nose and I say, "Do you feel sick?" he'll say, "no," because he is *not* going to vomit. The word "sick" is associated only with vomit. And if I say, "You hurt here in your face because you have a runny nose," that will also not work. He reserves "hurt" for bleeding. So I have to find a word that will describe what it is like to have a cold. But the word "cold" won't work, because to Ben "cold" is the temperature outside. If I cannot come up with the right word, that can make him frustrated. You have to find something that will describe to him how he feels, and then he can communicate back to me, "Yes, that is how I feel and now I feel better because I have a word for it." I don't know if that is true with other kids, but for him that is really important. [Biklen 1987, 24–25]

Not all conversations with Ben work even this well. When family members don't know what is on Ben's mind, whether it is something that pleases him or troubles him, they sometimes try to get him to fill in the blank. For example, Sue or Bob might say, "Boy, you really feel happy (or mad) because ———" and hope that he will finish the sentence. But this strategy can backfire if he gets frustrated with his inability to be understood when he is not communicating verbally. Nearly all of Ben's small amount of verbal communication is prompted by what another person says, which he will often repeat.

Sometimes, even when Ben communicates clearly, his environment does not respond in the way that he wants it to. His mother describes such an instance. Ben went to the telephone and began to speak into it, saying, "Sherry, come home now!" Sherry is one of his sisters, who at the time was away at college; obviously, he missed her. When the phone did not respond, he started to hurt himself, beating his head with his own fists. "Imagine his frustration," his mother explains. "He did what he was supposed to do, he said what he was supposed to, and it still didn't work." The question for the family is how to respond to Ben's frustration. If left to his own devices, he will "sit there and scream and cry and smack himself," so the family tries to create some alternative to his feelings of frustration. In this case, Bob and Sue talked about the fact that Sherry was away at school and that she *would* be returning but not right away. Not sure that Ben grasped the idea of time, they got out a calendar and put a picture of Sherry on the date that she would be coming home. With Ben, they checked off each day until Sherry arrived.

As interesting as such interactions appear to an observer, they are only part of the Lehrs' support for Ben. They have always insisted that Ben attend regular schools and take classes with nondisabled students, even though this has meant taking him to a school system in another town that would accept him. Also, like Mary Lou Accetta, Sue and Bob Lehr keep track of Ben's accomplishments. He has attended typical schools all of his life, from preschool on; students his age know him and initiate conversations with him, trying to get him to acknowledge what they are doing together (for example, working in the school office, filling the soda machine in the staff lounge, making a design in art class, lifting weights in gym). A nondisabled classmate tells his parents how well Ben is doing in learning to use money, and his classmates feel comfortable sitting next to Ben at the lunch table, walking with him, or guiding him in a group activity. His school activities include art class, home economics (he likes to sew), physical education. Right now he seems not to like physical education, perhaps because he does not like the activities or perhaps because he does not like the student with whom he is paired; his parents and teachers are struggling to figure this out.

Now that he attends a middle school, Ben spends two mornings a week at a job: He works in the lumber section of a large home and garden store. He spends another two mornings a week shopping for lunch foods, going to the library, going to the bank to cash his check from his store job, and shopping or eating out. He participates in several after-school activities as well, including two afternoons a week at a community center's teen program, one afternoon in the Spanish Club, and one afternoon during the winter months at cross-country skiing. He does not speak Spanish, but he was invited by the Spanish Club members to join because when they were building a haunted house as a fund-raising project, one student remembered Ben's interest in hammering and mentioned it to the club's adviser.

When he first went to middle school, Ben's behavior deteriorated badly. He pulled out so much of the hair on the back of his head that his parents got him a crew cut, which fortunately was in style at the time. He would press his fingers on his temples and grind them back and forth until his temples bled; his parents thought he looked as if he had been in an auto accident. He would make a fist and punch his cheek or the back of his neck, or slap himself on the neck until he looked bruised. He pinched his sides, lifting his shirt to pinch himself until he bled. He pulled at his navel. And he hit his head on the wall. It was extremely difficult to stop him. "If you managed his environment so that he didn't have anything to hit his head on," recalls his mother, "he would try to hit it on you, or he would get down on the floor and hit his head there. If you stopped him from hitting his head, he would hit his arms against the wall." He did not do these things constantly, but he did them enough to create serious difficulty and concern for his teacher and his parents. They met often to try to figure out what was wrong. Perhaps he was just anxious about being in a new environment with a new teacher. It was hard to tell.

Eventually they decided that Ben was trying to tell them to "give him more space." When the year began, the new teacher at the middle school had thought that the best approach would be to give Ben lots of structure, stay close to him, and be demanding. The teacher or an aide was always nearby, giving clear but possibly too directive instructions: "You will do this" and then "You will do that." Aside from the self-abuse, there were other signs that Ben was resisting the demands. He would turn his head away and even verbalize his feelings, which was unusual for him: "No more Rick today." Rick was his teacher.

As teacher and parents relaxed their demands, Ben's self-abuse subsided. Occasionally he would even correct himself, saying, for example, "You need to get under control." Here he was repeating a phrase that he had heard others say to him. Sue and Bob began to give Ben more autonomy, but at the same time they tried to help him manage his own behavior by cues in the form of questions. If he was about to pull on someone, they might say, "Where do your hands go?" or "Do you want to put your hands in your pockets?" Whenever he seemed out of control, they began a question, "Do you need . . . ?" The combination of giving him physical distance from them and giving him choices worked. There were other strategies as well. For example, at school, Ben needed to be able to walk from one class to another without bothering other people in the halls. This was nearly impossible for him. He didn't like to walk with his hands in his pockets, so that would not work. Then his teacher arranged for him to place one hand on another student's shoulder—a student who felt comfortable and confident with Ben—and one hand against the hallway wall. Before long, students were volunteering to assist Ben: "Look, I'm going to walk with Ben," they told their teacher, or "Ben never hurts me; I can do it."

In language development, Ben still has trouble with his pronouns. He regularly replaces the word "I" with the word "you," probably a function of repeating phrases he hears. Sue Lehr explains the problem and their remedy:

> "I's" and "you's" are real hard. So with him all we do now is—in fact we have the kids at school do it too; he knows the right way to say it but he is very lazy—we just put our hand on our chest, say "remember you know that." And if that doesn't work, sometimes you can just give him a real frustrated look, like a frown, and he will look back at you, as if to say, "I know I am supposed to correct this." That started initially with us tapping his chest lightly and saying, "We are talking about this person." Now it has gotten to where we can do it just a little bit.

In general Ben seems to learn well when people look for things that he is capable of doing and then teach these activities in small steps, ensuring that he will have opportunities to be successful.

His difficulty with language as well as some of his behaviors make social relations problematic for Ben. Sue explains:

> In junior and senior high, kids hang around in small groups. Their conversations are fast paced and are about either teachers or girls, if it's boys talking, or about sports. Special kids don't have that repertoire. Particularly at the high school level, I think it's hard to involve special kids in a teen network. In some cases if they have grown up together, that will change. But it is real difficult. Teenagers go to movies. Well, if you have a kid who can't attend to a two-hour movie and then can't talk about it, they're not going to be included in that network. So how do you put that piece in place? What piece do you come up with so that they are included? I don't have an answer for that yet.

Ben doesn't initiate relationships in a traditional sense but needs his social life structured for him. For one year, Sue and Bob Lehr hired three high school students to take turns "hanging out" with Ben after school. Two were basketball players and one was on the wrestling team. One of them would meet Ben at his bus each day and spend the afternoon with him. It generally worked out well, though Sue relates one incident that suggests a limitation to the arrangement:

> I would come home and Joe would be watching television and would have no idea where Ben was or what he was doing. Ben could be wreaking havoc, and Joe wouldn't know it. Yet Ben liked Joe. One day I came home to find my largest bowl (institutional size) mounded with flour, shortening, cinnamon, brown sugar, and sugar. I keep everything in gallon jars. Ben had emptied all the jars into the bowl. So I said to Joe, "What is this?" And he said, "Ben's making cookies." So I said, "Oh, where's the recipe?" And Joe said, "Recipe? I thought Ben knew how to make cookies." Ben was stirring this big mess.

The good part of this scene, of course, was that Joe was treating Ben very much as a peer. As Sue recalls the event, "they were enjoying themselves and Ben had a big grin." Ben has not seen Joe in quite some time, but he often says, "See Joe today."

As for paying the students, Sue views it as necessary and therefore justified: "I'm willing to give them money to hang out with Ben," she explains. "Eventually they are going to get to know him, and they are going to develop a relationship with him. But they're not going to initiate it, and Ben's not going to initiate it." Realistically, she says, "it will never happen if I don't get that started somehow." The result is that Ben knows several people around town and they know him. At the local grocery store, one of the three students hired to spend afternoons with him greets him and talks to him; similarly, the store owner has taken an interest in him. And when he goes with his parents or sisters to a high school basketball game, Ben frequently gets big waves from some of the students.

One student who considers himself Ben's close friend was not recruited by Ben's parents. Tim got to know Ben in middle school. He has been abused and neglected in his own home and has been only moderately successful in school. Sue Lehr thinks that he likes Ben's company in part because Ben appreciates him but also because Ben does not make demands on him. At times Tim can be overpowering and negative, giving Ben orders: "Don't do that. Stop doing that." Since Ben responds poorly to negative commands—he prefers questions and choices—he can get to a point of wanting Tim to leave; he will say, "No more Tim." Tim may be simply passing along a style of relating that has been part of his own background, but when Ben says he wants him to leave, Tim does recognize the futility of being negative with Ben. In fact, he catches on to strategies for dealing with some of Ben's obstinacy. For example, one day when Tim was visiting, he went outside and began taking basketball shots. Then, as if he had suddenly remembered where he was and his responsibility to his host, he came back in the house and asked Ben if he would like to play. Ben didn't want to. So Tim said, "Okay, what do you want to do?" After Ben responded, Tim made a deal: "Good, we'll do that after we shoot five baskets." So they went and played basketball first and then did what Ben wanted to do.

Sue and Bob Lehr have often heard the remark "Oh you must be so patient; I don't know how you manage with Ben." They know that special education teachers hear similar comments. But they believe that such statements really mean "Why do you do this? It cannot be worth the effort. I would not want to do it." For them, Ben does not need patience as much as he needs people who see him as a worthy person and as someone who deserves to be understood, not punished. The idea of patience suggests "putting up with" or "suffering" another person. Of course, there is a measure of that in raising any child, and certainly in raising a child who can be self-abusive to the point of smashing his head through four windows in a week. But the Lehrs cannot see Ben simply as a burden to be tolerated. He is always someone they love and someone to be interpreted: What does it mean when he smashes a window with his head or tries to cut his arms?

To them it does not make any sense at all to get angry with Ben: "Teachers are often still intimidated by kids who are self-abusive. . . . They do not know how to respond. And if a student pinches them or hurts them or another student, they might take it personally. But they really shouldn't. That person just happens to be there . . . the wrong person at the wrong time." Certainly, one could try to contain Ben with rules, with punishments and rewards, but could such a person come to understand what Ben is feeling and what he wants? His mother explains the choice: "It is easier to be a jailer than it is to be an educator. It is easier to confine and isolate and to say 'Stop doing these things' than it is to say 'How can I help you change?'" People who are willing to get to know Ben have proved that they can interact with him and that he responds. He is not *just* a person who abuses himself or who communicates in unusual and limited ways. He is also a person who likes company, who seems to appreciate certain people and certain activities more than others, and who can communicate his preferences, if not always in socially appropriate ways. His family, his teacher, his schoolmates, and others have demonstrated that with support he can participate.

Disability: Only One of Several Challenges

Tommy Mason's disability does not represent the only or even the major challenge to his family. To understand how the other members experience Tommy, one must understand the family's circumstances.

When I called Martha Jane Mason one day to get together to talk about her son Tommy, she turned the subject to what for her was more pressing: drug dealing in her Syracuse neighborhood and drug use by one of her sons. She asked me to join her at a meeting at the Magnolia Housing Project Coffee House on O'Shea Street.

That afternoon Martha Jane and I attended the second gathering of a group of African American mothers united to fight drugs and to find support to deal with their sons and daughters who were drug users. In the coffeehouse, a converted apartment in the public housing unit, a dozen mothers sat around the room on couches, easy chairs, and folding chairs. Maria, who had called the meeting, began by telling about her experiences with her daughter: "I've been going through a lot lately. My daughter is sixteen and she's an alcoholic. She dabbles in cocaine. At least I hope she just dabbles," she said almost tearfully. "Nothing I say seems to work. And I don't know what to do. I don't know if I should be tough or what."

"Be tough," another mother counseled her. "You be tough. I don't care if you call it tough love or just doing what you have to do but you gotta do it. You gotta throw her out, lock her out. She wants you to pay for it [drugs], but she's got to pay for it. You'd be paying for the rest of your life. Tough is all you've got. That's the only thing that saved me. I'm an addict. I've been up so high and down so low. I got out of rehabilitation on September 13th, and I've been straight ever since."

Rosella joined in with advice on how to handle the daughter. "You let her in and have the warm bed and the good food, and she'll be back out there the next night. And you'll be paying for her habit for twenty years. I know. I was an addict for twenty-two years, on cocaine. I've got six kids too; the oldest is eighteen, the youngest five, and I've seen it all. I've been off drugs for a year. You gotta be tough because those drugs don't take no days off. They're there on your bad days; they're there on your good days; they're there on your days off too."

"Yeah," Tarra chimed in. "Yeah, 'I had such a good day, I deserve something for it.' Shiiit, I know where you're coming from. I've been there too. I was an addict and been off for six years."

"I know that's right, but it's hard," replied Maria. "I've got to stop my daughter. I took the alcohol out of the house, got rid of the Jack Daniels and the beer. But everywhere she goes, it's there [liquor and drugs]."

Tarra blamed society for her daughter's plight: "You're right. We got to stop not just the demand; we got to stop the supply and the demand. Coors comes in here and wants us to drink their beer. Television pushes all that stuff. They create the expectations that it's cool, but they don't come in here and hire our people, and they're not here when we need rehabilitation."

"That's my complaint," Martha Jane interjected. "One of my sons is doing good. He works for the state, and the state insurance paid for his treatment and he's still working. My other son—I've got two on drugs—my other son's not doing too good."

"Does he have a job?" Maria asked.

"No. That's what I'm saying. He worked for the state too, but he lost his job. And my insurance won't cover him. He's over twenty-one. I called St. Park and Congrove and Street House [drug treatment centers], but I can't pay. They say I can't get him in. He could go up to the hospital, but I've seen how they treat folks. They treat us people like dogs. They see somebody's an alcoholic or on drugs and treat them like dogs. I don't care what somebody's on, it's not right to treat them like dogs. Addiction's like any other disease, diabetes, heart problem, whatever, it's not right to treat a person like a dog. I know what they do. I've been there on a Saturday night. They throw you in a room and that's it."

The group talked on, mainly about their personal experiences and the difficulty of getting treatment but also about the need to coalesce as a group of African American mothers—to their knowledge there were no other African American mothers' anti-drug groups in the city. They wanted to be more than a parent-to-parent support group. They wanted to take action to stop the sale of drugs in their neighborhoods. They were angry that drug dealers seemed to be able to sell their products so openly and widely: "The police chief says they're making a lot of arrests," Maria reported, "but they [the pushers and dealers] don't stay in jail very long. For one thing, the jails are full. Actually, they're overcrowded. Another thing, and I don't know if it's true or not, some people say the big pushers got connections high up and so they don't go to jail. I think we need to find that out. And we need to pressure the politicians."

Mrs. Johnson, Rosella's mother, complained that if they lived in the suburbs they would not be having such a problem, because neighbors would be on the phone to the police at the very instant they spotted a dealer; here they were afraid to report. Martha Jane agreed with her: "I was warned by my neighbors, 'They'll burn down your house if you go after them [dealers and pushers].' I said, 'Fine, I'll collect my $8,000 insurance and get out of here.' Martha Jane isn't going to keep quiet. I don't care. I kept calling the police and the DA and the politicians, and they're off my corner." After she spoke, the others congratulated her; they nearly cheered.

As the group talked more about the need to take political action to get rid of the pushers, Martha Jane leaned over and whispered to me about what it had been like to walk to the neighborhood store. The pushers "come up to you and they bump your arm like this" (she tapped the outer side of her wrist against mine). "'You want some? I got the good stuff. Had your stuff today?' like that. They're there [in the street] from the time they get up in the morning to the time they go to sleep at night, everyday, don't matter the weather, cause that's their business." The meeting ended about fifteen minutes later, after everyone agreed to meet again in a couple of weeks.

Martha Jane has been fighting for one thing or another for a long time. Forty years ago she lived in Georgia, where she walked everywhere she needed to go rather than ride in the back of a segregated bus. Twenty years ago she was picketing for civil rights in the north. Seventeen years ago she was battling her school district to enroll her son.

Her fight for Tommy's education resembled other battles she has fought over the years. When she called the district offices, she was told that there was no program for students with severe disabilities, and Tommy was classified as retarded, blind, and physically disabled. She found the district's claim upsetting and more than a little puzzling. The fact that her son had severe disabilities only made her concern for his education more urgent. Besides, she reasoned, she had no choice about whether or not to have him in school. She had a family to raise, two jobs, and no discretionary income; in other words, if she were forced to stay at home to care for Tommy during school hours, she would have to go on welfare. Although she did not know it at the time, Tommy was one of nearly a million students being excluded from public schools on the pretext that they were too disabled or that programs were simply unavailable (Children's Defense Fund 1974). Yet his mother knew that if he had had no disability and had not been in school, the district would have begun neglect and truancy proceedings against her and Tommy. She told the school officials that she would not back down on its obligation to educate her son. It would not be the first time or the last that Martha Jane's vision conflicted with society's standard practice.

Tommy had been unconscious in the hospital for four months following an accident, when at the age of five he was hit in the head by a ricocheting bullet. His mother visited him daily:

> I would shake him and talk to him. Even though he was unconscious, I thought he moved his lips. But everyone else, including my husband, thought it was my imagination. Then one day it wasn't my imagination. I was ready to leave, and I said, "Tommy, see you tomorrow. I love you." I gave him a kiss on his forehead, and he says something back. It sounded like "puh." I nearly yelled. "I heard a sound," I hollered. I ran down to the waiting room and told my husband. He said, "Oh hon, you're imagining things." And I said, "No, I'm not." We went back to Tommy's room, and I says, "Tommy, you can't let me down, you have to do it for Dad." So we really worked together. Tommy did it again. He made a sound.

When it came time for him to leave the hospital, the doctors encouraged Martha Jane to "place" Tommy at Central State School, an institution for people with mental retardation. She refused. "I was determined. When the doctor said take him to Central, I said, 'No, you send yours to Central, I'm taking mine home.'"

At home, Tommy had to be taught "everything" all over again. He had to learn to sit up, to eat, to speak, to walk—everything. This was a trying time for his mother. She had just separated from her husband and had sole responsibility for raising seven children. Tommy is the second youngest. She marks his development with pride: "He can get in the bathtub with instructions; I can remember when he first had braces . . . his first steps. If I ask him a question, he'll think about it and answer me." And she wonders aloud, "If I were just going to accept it [the school district's response], 'Well we don't have any place for him,' what might have been?"

The school district never did accept Tommy, who was deemed unable to benefit from the district's programs. The director of pupil services finally assigned him to a private special school for severely disabled students only. Upon graduation, he entered a "day treatment center" where he plays games, sits around in a large room for part of each day, and takes walks in the community with staff members. All the people at the day treatment center are presumed to be too severely disabled to work or to attend recreation centers with people who do not have disabilities.

Martha Jane credits Tommy's success at walking and talking to her work with him at home to retrain him, to her network of supporters (a combination of neighbors, family members, priests, and sympathetic social workers), and to her faith: "My faith always kept me going and my faith in Tommy." At the same time, she credits Tommy with bolstering her spirits when she has been feeling down. When her husband of twenty-five years left and when one of her sons was imprisoned, Tommy "would give me faith," she says. "He says, 'Now Mom, God is taking care of it now. You better not cry.' I says, 'You're right, Tommy.' He is an inspiration to me."

People in his neighborhood know Tommy. Kids on the block wave and say "Hi, Tommy" when they pass him. Family members take turns going out for walks with him. In the morning when he climbs on the bus to go to the treatment center, he says to the bus driver, "Morning." Martha Jane says, "Have a good day, Tommy," and he responds, "You too." If Martha Jane needs to go out for an errand, Tommy will say, "Mom, where you going?" Occasionally, he will go with her to Mass.

Given the acceptance and involvement that Tommy already enjoys in his community, Martha Jane smiles when she talks about the day treatment center's seemingly artificial approach to community participation; she also recognizes its staff members have not made any effort to find out about his family life and role in the community.

They were trying to decide if everyone should walk in their own neighborhood so they could get to know their own neighbors. That's good too, but why can't they walk in other people's neighborhoods? You know, don't limit me. Don't fence us in. You know Tommy does walk in his neighborhood. He walks with me, his brothers, his sisters. We take turns. We do go on picnics. Occasionally, we go to Ponderosa [a restaurant]. He always has gone out. . . .

There aren't any problems because we won't let there be problems. People know they better not say anything discriminating against Tommy because I give them a look that says he's part of me. So we go out with the family and my daughter-in-laws. He's part of us. If I feel like I don't want to make dinners and I have extra pennies to spend, I'm not going to have a sitter to sit with Tommy simply because we want to go out. He needs that. Same thing for parks. If we go out on a family gathering or with friends, we take Tommy. That's why he responds this well.

Throughout the years of caring for Tommy, Martha Jane has faced many difficult family struggles. One of her sons was tried and convicted for murder. Throughout the trial, Martha Jane went to the courtroom daily and met regularly with her son's defense lawyers, trying to find evidence that would save him. He was sentenced to twenty-five years to life in a state penitentiary. Another son had a mental breakdown. Her second husband left her. Two sons have had persistent bouts with drugs. Her house caught on fire, leaving her with severe burns. And during the interviewing for this book, her daughter was arrested in connection with a drug-pushing ring, and an acquaintance stole several checks from her.

Despite this virtual avalanche of difficulties, Martha Jane kept active in her community. For example, one afternoon while we were discussing Tommy, a former city legislator dropped by Martha Jane's house at her request. She asked him to influence the local poverty agency to increase the staff at her neighborhood agency's office so that it could better handle the needs of an influx of homeless and poor people. Several months later she helped organize a neighborhood meeting with the school superintendent. Such advocacy has been a constant part of her life.

Over the years, Martha Jane says she has needed only one major form of assistance other than school and adult programs for Tommy: an aide to assist in getting Tommy ready to leave the house in the morning and to be at the house with him in the late afternoon until she can get home from her job as a teaching assistant or from family errands:

> They're supposed to get him out of bed in the morning . . .
> make breakfast, pancakes and syrup, eggs and bacon and
> things like that, toast. If it's late, there's cereal. They do his
> sheets and laundry. Once a week I like the bed washed down.
> He has a hospital bed. He helps himself in the bathroom. Just
> tell him, "The water's fine. You can get in. Now sit down
> Tommy. . . . Now I'm going to shampoo your hair." Then dry
> him off, put on the Attends [adult diaper], dress him, brace on
> one leg, sneaks or boots, depends on the weather because he
> walks from the porch to the bus. I like to have his chair
> washed once a week. That's it. Oh yes, his lunch is packed.
> They make the lunch, peanut butter and jelly, franks, bolo-
> gna—he doesn't like tuna fish—danish, donuts to throw in
> with the two sandwiches. He's a man, so he needs a lot.

Martha Jane rattles off the duties of an aide with perfect familiarity. When Tommy comes home, the aide meets his bus, greets him— "Hi Tommy, how was school today?"—and makes sure he finds the railing on the front steps as he goes into the house. The aide then checks the Attends and assists him with a second bath.

Martha Jane points with pride to the fact that in the twenty-one years Tommy has had a disability, he has never had a problem with his skin breaking down from being dirty. Aide services and her own persistent watchful care have kept Tommy in good health.

The services of aides has been uneven, however, and the turn-over rate is high: Aides find higher-paying jobs, go to school, move away, decide they do not like the work, get fired for absenteeism, or have other problems. A year ago, for example, when Martha Jane was recovering from open-heart surgery, an aide announced that she was not able to come during the Fourth of July weekend. That put additional pressure on the family. Then, over a period of several weeks, another aide neglected to do some of the required tasks. Martha Jane describes the difficulties:

> I had surgery at the end of June. Thanks be to God I come
> home. I didn't know what was going to happen on the
> Fourth. I was too sick to bother. I come home and I would be
> coughing. I had this pillow for coughing. I don't expect the
> aide to take care of me, but I do expect her to take care of
> him. Then one aide didn't want to give him his bath in the af-
> ternoon. She didn't want to do her work. One time, Carter
> [Tommy's brother] asked, "Did you feed Tommy?" She
> hadn't. That's what I need and want him to do. He's supposed
> to watch after his brother. Well, she made him pancakes . . .
> [and then] complains [about Carter telling her what to do].
> We all get basically lazy sometimes, you know, but you know
> not each day. Like one or two days, you say to yourself,
> "Maybe she overlooked that; maybe she didn't want to do that
> today." But if she overlooked that two or three days in a row,
> I'm going to say something.

Dealing with the service can be a problem in itself. An aide may respond to criticism by quitting instantly, leaving the family without help. And complaints raise questions about how Martha Jane treats Tommy and the aides. Her report about the aide who neglected several of her responsibilities, including changing and bathing Tommy—which caused him to arrive dirty at the day treatment center—resulted in a home visit by social services officials,

and Martha Jane felt that she was being investigated. She tried unsuccessfully to call three different friends to come to the house to
be with her in the meeting with the caseworkers. The social services
department report painted a picture of Martha Jane as unable to
give guidance for Tommy's care and intimated that she was the
problem. They made no acknowledgment of her continuing efforts
on his behalf, her fighting to get him in school and arrange his
transportation, as well as her complete responsibility for his care for
twenty-four years without a vacation because the county would
provide no respite services other than placement in an institution.
The caseworker's report reads in part:

> The home situation was quite disruptive and Mrs. Mason ap-
> peared to have difficulty attending to the discussion at hand
> (She was caring for 5 grandchildren appearing to be under the
> age of 5 or 6 years and made several phone calls to outside
> contacts during the 45 minute home visit time.) She did not
> appear to be able to focus on the discussion or provide infor-
> mation adequate to this agency's staff to make an informed
> decision regarding aide service in the home. . . .
>
> She related an incident of Tommy losing his trousers when
> the aide was accompanying him to the bus to attend day care
> and that she had to assist the aide. . . .
>
> Until the phone call (by the agency) and home visit, none
> of these problems she had related were ever brought to the at-
> tention of this agency.

The social services department and Martha Jane Mason were at
an impasse. The department refused to continue the aide service,
insisting instead on giving the family's supervisory role to a nurse
who would come to the home more often. Martha Jane rejected
this change and requested continuation of the original form of assistance. She felt that her family was being portrayed as inadequate:
"They said my home was disruptive in their report. I had four or
five kids running around. I'm supposed to close my door to my
grandkids and my family? My family is my foundation. Family is
why Tommy is as well as he is today. Cause he know he's loved and
he's not going to be pushed into his bedroom simply because he

has handicaps. Either you accept him or you don't. Or you don't accept any of us." She wanted help in caring for Tommy, but she would not have her dignity impugned or her home taken over; above all she would not allow anyone to take over Tommy's care from her. She was stunned when a caseworker mentioned that "Adult Protective Services" might have to be called into her home—in her view, all because she had been critical of the aide service's inconsistency.

Martha Jane Mason's family has been beset by troubles: drugs, prison, psychiatric difficulties, health problems, and unemployment. Yet Martha Jane never allowed misfortune to justify her family's losing respect in her eyes. She views her family as a good family, if sometimes beleaguered. And despite his severe and multiple disabilities, Tommy is as stable a personality in the home as anyone. His care has become a unifying force—although certainly not the only one or even the central one for the family—and the basis for a network of friends to enter the family's life. If society did not respond to Tommy's needs, the family tended to see this as a breach of public responsibility. Martha Jane is as comfortable advocating for Tommy's aide services as she is for school reform or for drug enforcement and treatment.

Conclusion

No two families are alike, and the three discussed in this chapter differ in race, class, composition, and prevailing issues; their children's disabilities also differ in the type and severity. They present a range of the characteristics found in families that include people with disabilities, but they were not selected to represent specific demographic characteristics. It is not accidental, however, that all three families advocate the integration of people with disabilities into schools and society: Martha Jane Mason tried unsuccessfully to enroll her son in public school; Mary Lou Accetta adopted her son in part to help him escape an institution; the Lehrs bussed their son from the rural community that refused to educate him with non-disabled students to a community that would do so. They all point to their experiences as evidence that inclusion of the person with a disability is possible and that it "works." Moreover, they share elements of a philosophy of education and child rearing and of the individual's place in society, demonstrating that the vision of inclusion can cross class, ethnicity, and disability boundaries.

With a philosophy that recalls Freire's and Ashton-Warner's literacy frameworks, they approach their children with the intention of inquiring, not of labeling or domesticating. They look to understand why a child runs from a setting or a person, or bashes his head when the telephone gives no response; they treat self-abusive or hurtful or otherwise difficult behavior not as defining characteristics of the child but as instances of behavior chosen from among possible behaviors—and as changeable. Whatever their children's difficulties with communication, they nevertheless persist in looking for ways for them to make choices. They treat their children as people with whom they can have dialogue. In an educational sense, the children are the text; the families learn from them.

The centrality of disability to a family's life changes over time and with circumstances. Family income and ethnicity may influence the degree to which disability dominates a family's creative or coping energies, but they do not appear to be the only such factors. The manner in which a teacher spoke to Ben or a former institution staff person spoke about Mel caused disruption for them and their families. The absence of a school program for Ben in his home community and the discontinuance of aide services for Tommy focused family attention on those problems. Indeed, these and numerous other situations suggest that the family's experiences with disability are to a large extent shaped by society's ways of responding to disability.

Chapter III

Escape from Client Status

SOCIETY HAS a long history of treating people who have been classified disabled as clients whose duty it is to abdicate self-determination and other individual liberties. Nowhere is that clearer than in Justice Oliver Wendell Holmes's poetic and devastating defense of eugenics, the purported science of improving races and the human stock by management of heredity. Holmes wrote his opinion in the case of Carrie Buck (Buck v. Bell 1927), a young woman who had been incarcerated at a Virginia institution for the "feebleminded."

> We have seen more than once that the public welfare may call upon the best citizens for their lives. It would be strange if it could not call upon those who already sap the strength of the state for these lesser sacrifices. . . . It is better for all the world, if instead of waiting to execute degenerate offspring for crime, or to let them starve for their imbecility, society can prevent those who are manifestly unfit from continuing their kind. The principle that sustains compulsory vaccination is broad enough to cover cutting the Fallopian tubes. Three generations of imbeciles are enough. [274 U.S. 200]

Holmes wanted people with disabilities to serve their country by warranting that their future progeny would never burden society. In 1927, at the time of his decision, belief in a causal link between intellectual disability and criminality was popular, if unproven.

49

Holmes envisioned forced sterilization as a kind of vaccination, a way of preventing intellectual disability from spreading.

Holmes's statement denies Carrie Buck the chance to be like other people; like much of society, he saw Carrie Buck as *not* like other people, and hence he was willing to treat her unjustly. Eugenicists' ideas about forced sterilization have long since been invalidated and generally rejected (Gould 1981), but the status of people with disabilities as clients to whom society can mete out unusual treatment—including forced segregation—persists.

In direct contradiction to this perspective, some parents speak of wanting equal status for their children, by which they mean a place in schools and society. To find such a place, they believe, schools and society must change in some of the same ways that they have changed as a result of living with their children. Three main concepts dominate their vision: treatment of their children as individuals; support that does not subject them or their children to client status; and participation by their children in the family and in the culture. These three concepts and their corollaries set a context for inclusive education.

This chapter is based on interviews with the parents of the six families central to the book, interviews with eight additional families who were the focus of an earlier study on family support for children with a variety of severe and multiple disabilities (Biklen 1988), and interviews with selected other families that have been involved in the effort to achieve inclusive education.

Seeing the Individual

Children First

Like most parents, these parents view their children with disabilities as individual personalities; they do not impose labels or stereotypes. Whatever their previous perspective on disability, they came to this acceptance rather quickly as a result of living with their children. Bob Lehr recalls the decision of whether to keep Ben once he and Sue Lehr realized that the boy was "developmentally delayed." It was really not a decision at all: "After nine months, he was our kid. There was no way we could say, 'You're not our kid so goodbye.'" There is a similar sense of commitment and even enthusiasm in Mary Lou Accetta's comment that underneath the labels attached to her son Melvin she could see a "neat, bright kid." The parents talk about enjoying their children and family life. None of them subscribe to the notion that they would rather not have their children. When people say to her, "Oh your life must be so difficult," Rose Galati says, "But it's not." For Rose and Dominic, "our favorite times are when the four of us are by ourselves. Maybe we see that some of the stuff our kids have to go through is tough, so we don't see caring for them as tough."

Although not all parents adopt this attitude, many parents do choose inclusion, do view the child as an individual and as having *potential*. For example, several families who were part of the study on family support (Biklen 1988) demonstrate this optimistic parent perspective. Tasia, seven years old, has been classified as profoundly intellectually disabled. She is blind—she has no eyes. Her head has a large protrusion, an encephalocoele or sac about seven inches in diameter, filled with spinal fluid. She has good muscle tone in her legs and arms; indeed she looks healthy, even strong, although she is unable to sit up, stand, or walk. She needs total care, yet her foster mother (a single parent) speaks of teaching her self-toileting. She believes Tasia may be able to feed herself and may also learn to stand. Tasia came to this home from an intermediate care facility; prior to that she had been a resident in a nursing home. She is the kind of child one sometimes sees in an institutional infirmary.

Another "medically involved" child observed as part of that family support study had been diagnosed as anencephalic: that is, born without a brain. Semantha weighed three pounds and two ounces at birth; at age five she weighs twenty-one pounds. She has a shunt, or drainage tube, to control hydrocephalus. When she first entered the foster family, she was awake twenty-four hours a day and cried a lot. Her adoptive mother believed that she was probably irritable because the shunt was malfunctioning. Eventually, the mother persuaded medical doctors to examine and fix the shunt. Semantha's crying ceased. The foster mother describes Semantha as being expressive: "She's vocalizing, not quite laughing. And she's kicking her legs. She just started doing that a little while ago."

A third child in this study was labeled "medically fragile." He had a gastrostomy so that he could be fed directly via a tube to the stomach, a tracheotomy to aid his breathing, a colostomy to bypass his malfunctioning bowels, and one leg. When I first met him, he was outside his mother's home, riding a tricycle on the sidewalk with other children in his neighborhood. He was four years old at the time, and his mother was struggling with local education officials to secure a place for him in a local elementary school.

Parents have often been accused of not accepting their children's disabilities and therefore of not accepting their children. Parent narratives generally tell a different story. Parents do not usually feel any contradiction between being angry at their children's disabilities and lovingly accepting their children. One father explains that although he is not quite prepared to announce the disability equivalent of "black is beautiful," he does fully accept and love his son for who he is:

> It has been sixteen years since my kid's brain was damaged. I am not going to hop up out of bed every morning and say, "God, he's still retarded, let's go, it's great." If that's what acceptance means, then I don't think I will ever reach it. In a variety of ways as he gets older, problems change. There is a kind of, what another parent called "regret" about opportunities lost, potential unrealized. It's part of . . . the nature of him not being able to do things that I would like him to be able to do. [But] part of it is the inadequacy of social services. . . . Sure, I wish my kid were normal. What kind of respect for my son's value would I have if I didn't wish him normal?

This father's regret is punctuated by society's failure to celebrate his son as a deserving person, someone who should have access to typical schools, someone who should be able to get into restaurants or the movies in his wheelchair, and someone for whom it should be easy to get a sitter.

Underlying parents' insistence on seeing their children as children first, before the disability, is their understanding that being perceived as ordinary is a prerequisite for being allowed to be an ordinary participant. Parents want people to talk to their children without adding disability-related questions such as "Does he go to a special school?" or "How do you manage?"

Acceptance

Parents want people to care about their children. The parent of a child with severe autism remembers her trepidation about sending him to a nursery school. Although her son is now nineteen, she still remembers vividly that she "didn't have to beg for entry; they wanted us." The director and the teachers felt that Neil would be "good for the other children. They never made me feel I had to be grateful [to them] for taking him in." Further, "they made it abundantly clear that they enjoyed and cared for Neil. I never had that 'if only I were the child's mother' feeling that one can get from professionals."

Neil was not an easygoing child at that time. Whenever daily routines changed, he would cry. He wasn't interested in toys, and he did not play in groups unless coaxed and drawn in. On the playground he would do some things on his own, such as swinging or climbing the slide. He would not stay in the classroom with the other students at snacktime or for lunch. And he occasionally wet his pants. Yet the teachers spoke of his contributions, and the other children took an interest in teaching him; some of them liked being a helper for Neil. Neil's mother collected vignettes that demonstrated the acceptance he was finding:

> Once Erik, a boy Neil took a liking to, was working with Play-Doh. Neil was interested and watched him a long time. When Erik decided to do something else, Neil indicated to him, by placing his hand on his arm and leading him back to the table, that Erik should continue at play there. Erik acquiesced in this quiet request and was pleased to have been asked. How grateful I was for feelings of appreciation for Neil, feelings I just assumed the world granted my other children.

Neil's mother remembers crying at a teacher's conference when the teacher told her that other children liked Neil. Later, when he was

in public school, she recalls, he sometimes contributed to his classmates' welfare in one way or another:

> When he was in third grade he could spell better than many of
> the third graders. They were impressed that he could do that.
> I think they had a sense of his intellectual capacity, yet they
> thought, "Look how well he spells." Occasionally I have heard
> stories of kids being impressed by his effort when something
> was clearly so hard for him, yet he mastered it. As I watch at
> the pool, lots of those kids who come over, they are not swim-
> ming. They are in the water up to here, but they are not
> swimming. They are impressed that Neil can swim and that he
> is happy under the water.

Even though she believes that all students belong in public school
and that Neil's presence there is good for the other students, she
eagerly recites these instances of acceptance, almost as if to say,
"See, here's the evidence that what I said was true."

From the outside looking in, an observer might think that such
parents romanticize their children's progress. Indeed, most parents
do so from time to time. But what seems to occur is that these
parents come to know their children so well that they see changes
which others may not recognize or appreciate. The case of a child
named Sholanda is instructive in this regard. Sholanda, born
weighing ten pounds and one ounce, had a rare condition that left
her nasal passages blocked, was characterized by rapid aging and
retardation, and eventually required her to use a gastrostomy tube
for feeding and a respirator for breathing. Throughout her life her
condition seemed to get worse, yet her parents speak of her
strengths. They note with pride that she would begin throwing up
in the car each time they took her to the hospital, a possible sign of
her awareness: Perhaps she was resisting going to a place she regarded as hostile, they think. Although she had a tracheotomy, her
parents note that she tried to talk and to assert herself:

> I thought it was better her being at home than in the hospital.
> She would try to sit up. We tied her trach tube on, then she'd
> take it off. We'd tell her not to pull it out. My hand would be
> shaking, trying to get the tube back in, and she'd deliberately

hold her neck back like this so I couldn't get it in. I'd be fussing and she was laughing. Sholanda was in bed laughing. I'd say, "That ain't right." She just laughed and smiled and then she'd kick her leg. She was trying to talk, you know. She couldn't really talk. But she could holler. She also started scooting around. They thought she would do nothing, but she got to the point where she was scooting up under the bed. She started getting a little active until around her spine she had problems. The doctors told us we had to keep her in bed. So we did that, and she was getting mad.

She was stubborn. If she didn't want to be bothered by the teacher who was coming here, she would get to crying till you let her have her way. We weren't sure if she could see, but her hearing would follow you wherever you were.

Kevin, Sholanda's father, seems to have found a quality in Sholanda to offset each of her difficulties: she was blind, but she could hear; she could not talk, but she could holler; she was in pain, but she could laugh; she could do very little, but she could get her way.

Not long after having an appendectomy, Sholanda died. But her father recalls her time with the family as a good time: "She definitely knew where she was at. When she heard her sisters, she would smile. She was in a lot of pain. You know, man, she had a lot of problems. But just having her here and you know, just to show her that we loved her, you know, and for the short while, I thank God for that." Such remarks bespeak admiration and certainly acceptance. Serious health problems, extremely difficult behavior, severe intellectual disabilities are all problems to be accommodated and to some extent overcome. It is not Pollyannaish to say, even, that families who take such a view see progress and hope where many people less connected with their lives might imagine only tragedy, despair, and disappointment. Sholanda's father typifies this attitude: "When she was in Children's Hospital they told us a lot of things, like 'she'll never do this anymore, and she'll never be able to do that anymore, she'll never be able to do this.' Well, if that didn't destroy the confidence, we still believed. No, it didn't destroy the confidence. I had seen different."

Even a family that is more discouraged with its situation than

most may view its own efforts at inclusion as worthwhile, if difficult. The parents of twenty-one-year-old Matthew, who has been
labeled severely autistic, are concerned that he is still incontinent,
still groans a lot, and does not have a lot of things to do. They are
worried about his future, what will happen to him when he is no
longer eligible for school and when he needs a place to live, perhaps a group home. But the way this family approaches his future,
wanting to guarantee that he will be in a residence that will provide
him with warmth, caring, and training, suggests that the parents
believe he is doing as well as he is because of how he has been
treated by them. In other words, had he not lived at home, he
could be worse off, more self-abusive; he might engage in more
self-stimulatory behavior. This family showed me the device, a
board with pictures, with which Matthew is able to communicate a
few simple things, like "food" and "play." They told me about his
ability to ride as a passenger on the family motorcycle. They have a
short inventory of things he *can* do.

In living together, family members develop sensitivity to one
another. As we have already seen, this sensitivity includes the ability
to interpret nonstandard (nonverbal) communication. One foster
parent describes such an instance:

> Toni can say one word. She can raise her hand to say yes.
> Kerry will say, "Some juice please, Mom." As soon as she says
> that, Toni will make a loud noise. So I'll ask her if she wants
> some juice, and she'll raise her hand. A couple of months ago
> we had supper and we got done eating and Kerry said, "More
> spaghetti please." As soon as Kerry said that, Toni, who was
> sitting between Dad and me, made loud noises. I said, "You
> want more spaghetti?" Then up shot her hand. Now, when
> Toni gets off the school bus [or is gotten off in her wheel-
> chair], and the minute I pick up my teacup, she'll start with
> the noises. That's your clue to ask if she wants a drink. So
> she's figuring out ways to get her point across.

Unfortunately, the fact that a parent can understand what a
child wants does not always guarantee that it can be provided. The
typical experience of people with disabilities is atypical treatment,

not easily combatted. A mother empathizes with what her son, who has Down syndrome, faces daily:

Chris has gone through a lot of pain in his lifetime because his handicap is obvious, and I mean he gets on the bus and people say, "Well, isn't he. . . . " It doesn't matter what he does; people just look at him. He has always got to deal with that. Even when he was a little kid and got in trouble, it was [said by others] that it was because he was retarded. He couldn't just be a little kid who could get in trouble.

Of course, parents learn not to take special notice of how their children look or, at least, to see past appearance. One mother explains how she learned this lesson in the delivery room:

[The obstetrician] came over to the table and she said, "Susan, I don't know how to tell you this." And I said, "What?" She said, "I think he has Down syndrome." And I thought, "Shit." And then she said, "But the thing is, Susan, it doesn't matter," she said. "He still needs you. He needs you to love him. He has all the same needs. You were planning on breastfeeding. You better get started." She just kept going and going. I lay there and thought, this is one hell of a lady here.

This almost matter-of-fact, everyone-is-as-important-as-everyone-else attitude eventually becomes natural for people with disabilities and their parents. As the example of the obstetrician suggests, it can also become natural for others. Rose Galati hopes that it will become natural for everyone:

There are some people who have had absolutely no contact with people who are disabled. You can tell. You know, the jaw dropping open. It's not a nice kind of thing. It's not nice for Maria. We get pretty nasty sometimes. There are times when if someone is looking at Maria, I turn the wheelchair around and go straight for them. It's bad and I shouldn't do that, but we do. You know it kind of shocks them. Basically what I'm saying is, "Don't gawk at my little girl." . . .
    Any child who is in school where Felicia and Maria are

won't react the same way in the plaza. A lot of times if a child
comes along and pretty much ignores them, you know that
somewhere in their background they have had some experience
[with disability]. . . .

   If we're standing in a [checkout] line, we're standing in
line. Maria's not any different than anyone else.

It is not that Rose fails to see that Maria does not talk or walk and
that in these and other ways she is significantly different from other
children. Rather, by saying Maria is the same, she means that Maria
is not bad, that she does not deserve to be made fun of or stared at,
and that she wants what other people want, to experience everyday
things.

Support

Can people receive support and still not be cast in the role of perpetual clients? At the heart of the uneasiness that often attends pro-
fessional-client relationships is inequality—of status, power,
knowledge, experience, and authority. The term "client" derives
from the root word *cliens,* meaning "follower." When parents speak
of wanting support, they *do* envision a role for professionals as well
as for ordinary citizens, family members, and friends. But in accepting support, they are unwilling to abide unequal standing. Therein
lies the definition of the kind of support they seek.

The Right to Argue about or Refuse Treatment

   When the Lehrs first discovered that Ben's unusual behaviors
constituted a disability, they were eager to help him. Naturally,
they turned to professionals. But when they sought advice for Ben,
they were made to feel that *they* were the ones who needed treatment: "They treated us as clients. Us, clients. We were offered therapy for ourselves. They told us that we were having a traumatic
experience. But we weren't going through that at all. We resented
being treated as clients. We were really quite upset. They didn't tell
us what we could do [for Ben], and that's what we needed. In part,

maybe they didn't know what to do. But they never said that."
Several years later Ben's parents secured copies of those professionals' records, only to discover that they had been documented as
"pushy parents," the kind who would not be satisfied until they had
gone from one diagnostician to another, looking for a better, more
precise diagnosis. Bob sees that characterization as a stereotype:
"We weren't like that, and we haven't done what they said we
would do."

Some families are forced to undergo psychological exams as preconditions for receiving support. One parent describes her surprise
at having such a requirement imposed on her before being allowed
to bring her son home from the hospital: "I couldn't figure out,
why me. They were trying to see what type of people we were and
if we could handle Nicky, if we could handle the problems that
would come up, to see if we'd fall apart, end up in the crazy house.
I just answered his questions. Hey, he's our son. Whatever it takes,
we're going to do. I overcame that obstacle. You just go with the
punches."

When Mary Lou Accetta decided to take Melvin out of the institution and to adopt him, staff from the institution warned her
that she might not know what he was "really" like, that underneath
his sometimes calm presence was a wild child ready to explode. Of
course, the truth is that she had already seen much of his wildness;
she simply interpreted it differently. The fact that she was willing to
prove her own assessment correct probably did much to mute professional criticism of her decision to adopt Mel.

The Galatis encountered even more severe reactions from professionals when they attempted to enroll Felicia and Maria in regular school classes. They were told in an authoritative way that
classroom integration was "just simply not in the best interests of
the children." They remember that one superintendent accused
them of "'using' our daughter Felicia and of 'raping the system.' He
said we were 'like Qaddafi.' Single-minded. We didn't care who we
hurt." Only after some educators and parents began to see positive
results did Rose and Dom feel somewhat vindicated: "We're not
treated like crazy people anymore. Now, if people argue with us,
they just say, 'We don't agree with you.'"

For some parents, conflict with professionals may reflect a difference in social status or a perceived difference in life-style. The parents of Sholanda feel that some professionals were prejudiced against them because of their working-class, poor, minority status. Kevin, the father, remembers his discussions with his wife, also named Sholanda, about whether they could raise their daughter at home:

> The doctors wanted to put her in a convalescent home and at one time we almost decided to put her into a home. One night I said, "Sholanda, now look, what do you think? I'm looking out for your welfare, baby. Whatever you want, I'm with you. It's me and you, okay? Sholanda, it's a job. It's twenty-four hours around the clock. What do you think?" She thought and she thought. And she said, "Kevin, I can do it. I can do it." I said, "Now, they're looking at you being emotional, Sholanda. There's a lot in it, Sholanda," I said; "are you capable of taking that kind of responsibility?" She said, "Yes, Kevin." That's the way it was.

At first, the doctors objected to their taking their daughter home. Hospital officials thought they were incapable of caring for the child. Kevin believes that the doctors were treating his wife as if she were not intelligent. He wanted the doctors to give his wife her "props"—proper respect. He was offended that they might think of her as simpleminded; he was furious that this perception could keep their daughter from them: "She [my wife] has got a little speech problem. She stutters a little bit. But that don't make her ignorant. That's why I said [to the doctors], 'Who are you to judge?' I say, 'She stutters a little bit; that don't mean nothing. That's not going to make it that she's not going to take care of her baby.'" Kevin and Sholanda describe the struggle to convince health and hospital officials of their ability to care for their baby as a series of arguments, each having more to do with stereotypes than with what kind of people they are or how they live: The health department worker "said my house is not up to par. So we just got the roof fixed, and they said they weren't sure I could take care of Sholanda. Then this lady comes to the house and said I was on drugs and I drink. Sir, I don't smoke. I don't drink. And I'm terrified of needles. I don't do nothing." Kevin recalls how he insisted on being treated with respect by the health worker:

> I called them, and I said, "Are you coming out here again?" She said, "Well, I want to come out to your place, but I'm wondering how you're going to act." I said, "Well, let me tell you. If you put me on the ropes, I'm going to bounce off to you. If you come here with sense, I'll talk to you with sense. You come here foolish, and I'm going to treat you like you're foolish. You know, either way you want. If you want to hurt me, I don't need no more pain. Cause I've got enough pain with my child sick. That's enough."

Each question of their competence and life-style meant a delay in bringing Sholanda home. The last delay meant that they could not bring her home by the Fourth of July holiday, the date they had hoped for. Eventually, they prevailed, probably because they had the backing of other professionals—family support workers— and also, as one caseworker remarked, because they were willing to "fight every little issue until they [health and hospital officials] can't say 'no' anymore."

Automatic Availability

Parents complain that raising a child with a disability in a culture that does not accommodate disabilities easily, consistently, or widely enough is tiring and sometimes demeaning (Featherstone 1981). They say that basic services such as blood for a son who has hemophilia, a wheelchair for a child who does not walk, and a modified curriculum for a student with a learning difficulty should be automatically available, not things for which you have to hold a telethon or other charity drive (Cutler 1981; Massie and Massie 1976; and Pieper n.d.). In their classic parent narrative *Journey*, Robert and Suzanne Massie vent their frustration with having to organize friends for blood donations for their son Bobbie, who has hemophilia. They resent having to thank the many community people who contribute blood to their son. Similarly, Betty Pieper feels personally guilty, as if she has failed her son, when she allows tele-thon officials to parade him on stage as an example of the children whom donors are aiding.

In the example of Sholanda, the parents' home was in an extreme state of disrepair when the baby was born. A family support worker describes it this way:

> They didn't have heat, the water was dripping from the faucets, they didn't have hot water. Their baby had a trach. They didn't have a vacuum. The roof was leaking. [There had been] terrible storms, and the back roof had collapsed on the house. The basement was terrible, filled with mold. The flooded basement ruined their furnace and their washer and dryer. The whole bit. You name it, they had it.

The father insisted that he would pay the state back for the improvements that were made on his house, but he was told there was no mechanism for reimbursements. Like the Massies and Betty Pieper, this family was forced to accept support in accordance with the rules of higher authorities.

Choice, Not Blind Acceptance

Parents want to be able to seek assistance of their choice and need, and not services that someone else has decided are best for them. One parent believes that the problem emanates from the need of professionals and organizations to justify their services:

> The school says "This is what you need," instead of admitting that there are a whole range of options; just because the school has a particular type of expertise, it offers that to all parents, says they all need it, and assumes that by offering it they are covering all needs. I find this approach rigid and inadequate. The person who provides the counseling tends to think all parents need counseling. The behavior person says, "I can straighten the family out by showing them how to work with the kid." The psychiatric social worker thinks the be-all and end-all of parent involvement programs is getting really effective parent groups going.

This parent admits that the programs may be valid—in other words, useful to certain parents—but he objects to the take-it-or-leave-it and you're-not-accepting-your-problems-if-you-don't-accept-the-treatment terms on which programs are presented to parents. He believes parents are evaluated on the basis of how they defer to professionals: "Acceptance as I understand it," he says somewhat sarcastically, "means nodding your head when the professional tells you what the program is. You are now very accepting of your child's disability. Acceptance gets translated into not making waves."

Parent-Professional Partnership

This parent envisions another relationship, one in which parents are peers with professionals, where parents can state their needs and have power to decide among real choices, or even to create choices that were not previously available. Other parents share that viewpoint. Joan Reidy, a parent-activist in Melbourne, Australia, helped fashion state policy that guarantees families the right to send children with a disability to the neighborhood school of their choice (Ministerial Review 1984; Chapter IV). The policy mandates parent participation in planning the child's educational program. Reidy regards the term "participation" as crucial to the meaning of the policy. "It's not parent involvement; it's parent participation. We want to share power not be 'involved' in someone else's power," she explained to me.

Parents want professionals who recognize that they need parents. "I think that teachers should be involved in parent groups not as a burden but as a way of recruiting support," one father explains. For example, he worries that when students with disabilities are mainstreamed in typical classes, special education teachers may become lost, unattached to any single area or aspect of the school. They need to keep in touch with other people who are working toward the same goals of integration and who have a strong commitment to the children; parents would be a logical support group. Of course, many schools have not accepted the idea of integration and see parents not as a potential resource but rather as people who place demands on them. One parent recounts another's struggles with such a school:

> I know a family in Eastern Hill with a five-year-old who has spina bifida—normal intelligence, great social networks, gets along fine in school. The mother had to fight like crazy to get him in a regular kindergarten. She is fighting to keep him in regular school next year. She will have a horrendous fight. The school officials want him to go forty-five miles away to a special class for kids labeled retarded so he can get his OT [occupational therapy] and PT [physical therapy]. She thinks that basically he will be able to learn to catheterize himself, and that would require some assistance; they just don't want to deal with that. It's just a classic example of administrative balking and poor attitude.

She is correct in calling it "poor attitude." It also reflects the idea that professional knowledge is in some way divorced from everyday—(that is, parental)—knowledge. Moreover, bureaucratic procedures can dictate practice, thus replacing reasoning or inquiry that involves parents and others who constitute the community of the school.

Unconditional Support

One father says it is typical to encounter "people who give advice and nosy ones who just want to know what is wrong and want a soap opera version of your life, in three minutes while you are standing in a grocery line." Not surprisingly, the people he feels most comfortable with have had experiences similar to his own:

> I didn't used to say this, but I really feel comfortable with parents of other handicapped kids. There are things I will talk about with them that I won't talk about very readily with other people. You drop your guard and say things like: "Oh yeah, he drives me crazy when he does things like that." If I said that to a professional, it gets written down in a permanent record, . . . even if that doesn't happen, I censor what I say. I

don't have to do that with parents. [With other people] I set up a guard. . . . It depends on the person.

The issue for this father is not whether he can accept his son. He can. Rather, the issue is whether anyone besides other families that include children with disabilities can accept his son and his attitudes about his son.

Individual Respect

When parents talk volubly about how they experience prejudice and stereotyping, they are actually reflecting on what they think it means to their children. They fear rejection and other forms of mistreatment for their children. Rose Galati is herself a teacher. When she enters a school, she interprets the way she sees other children treated as evidence of how her own children might be treated. She bridles when she hears a teaching assistant label children: "That's a one-on-one kid" or "this is a web larynx kid." She was furious with teachers who used a special education classroom as a place where they could smoke without having the students complain. When she observed a classroom in which a child with multiple physical and intellectual disabilities was left to lie on the floor for hours at a time, she wondered if the same thing might happen to her daughter Maria if she were a less militant parent:

> When you allow a kid to lie down like that . . . I mean the only program . . . for that kid was "relaxation therapy" in the morning with music and "relaxation therapy" in the afternoon with some range-of-motion exercises. Nobody ever moved this child. To me that was abusive. I know what was happening to his body.
>
> I looked at his wheelchair. Oh, I thought I had fought the issues on wheelchairs for *my* daughter. *That* wheelchair was incredible. He was sitting with his head back. His back was in a bowl. He legs were way out. And then, on top of that, his head rest was in a totally wrong position.
>
> And when he was being helped with lunch, the position they were trying to feed him in! Let me just say that I won't

be surprised if one day there is a news article that a child
choked at that school. It was disgusting.

Above all, Rose Galati has come to understand that children
with even severe or profound disabilities know when they are being
treated badly and will find a way to communicate that knowledge:
"Felicia went nuts last year. She is usually happy, but last year it got
to the point where she was crying every day. She could feel the
rejection last year, rough treatment, abrupt pulling her along [in
the hallway], talking to her harshly, abrupt commands." It is significant in this instance that Rose never adopts the point of view that
difficult behavior such as crying or not wanting to go to school is
an independent event. She assumes it means something. She never
assumes that Felicia and Maria do not feel or interpret their world
and their experiences, no matter how difficult it may be for them to
express themselves. Like Mary Lou Accetta with Mel or the Lehrs
with Ben, she tries to understand what each child may be trying to
communicate.

Encouragement of Initiative

Parents of children with disabilities often feel that they are pioneers. And they are. It is parents who have created large organizations to lobby for public education for their children. Some
parents, while they waited for public policy to catch up with their
forward thinking, established their own special schools. Later,
when public education became available but was not made universal, parents litigated on behalf of their children. Similarly, they often hear about new developments in education and bring them to
their local educators—though the parents frequently find that they
themselves must first prove the workability of such ideas.

Rose Galati, for example, located a physical therapist who could
advise the school on how to integrate Maria's therapy into the daily
routines of classroom life. Also, she found work that Felicia could
learn how to do through "community-based" instruction.

I was down at the beauty parlor talking to Mr. Malaka about
all of the job sites I had seen in other communities and the

courses I had taken on school integration and supported work. [Then I said to myself], "So come on Rose, you know all that, use it!" So after I had my hair done, I leaned over the counter and I said, "So Mr. Malaka, who does your windows?" And he said, "Well, I usually do." I said, "Oh, well you should have a break. How would you like someone else to come in and do it?" I don't know who he thought I might be talking about, but finally he said, "Are you talking about Felicia?" Then I explained that I was looking for a place where Felicia could come and practice and I was thinking about the big window up front. He didn't like that. He thought Felicia should be protected. He said, "What if its cold?" I said, "People work in the cold. Felicia can be cold." Well, he accepted her. Now, you'll see him go up to her and say, "Felicia, this is the way you do it." It's great.

Rose is already thinking ahead about other jobs. She says her own energy to pursue new avenues like the work placement at the beauty parlor expands in direct proportion to the support of other people. She would like the school to be as initiating as she is.

Sufficiency

When families encounter a paucity of support, the weight of responsibility for child rearing and advocacy with schools and other agencies typically falls on mothers. This fact reflects both societal expectations and the failure of many fathers to assume an equal role in child care. Interestingly, it is not uncommon for fathers to point out this inequity of effort and responsibility. For example, the father of Matthew, the young man who has severe autism, notes that although the entire family participates in supporting Matthew (when he was in the hospital for an operation, for example, his father, mother, and mother's sister split the hours of a day to be with him) the father is nevertheless occupied outside the home earning an income, and the mother bears most of the responsibility:

Matthew is nonverbal, non-toilet-trained, and very hyper. That noise he's making [a groaning hum] sometimes goes on for

months at a time. The non-toilet-training and noise are two
things that drive us up a wall. When it stops, you wonder
what he's doing. You become a little bit concerned. And not
sleeping at times, that's another problem. That's where we're
coming from. And Gertrude, my wife, obviously does the majority of the work taking care of Matthew.

Having a child with severe disabilities is not something parents
choose. Rather, it is something that comes upon them and to
which they adjust. An absence of support outside the home can
make the cost of such "adjustment" high. Matthew's father and
mother, for example, have not had a vacation in ten years. When I
interviewed them, they were planning a cross-country car trip with
their son, but were worried about whether it would work. Also,
they had decided not to move from their current house to a wealth-
ier neighborhood for fear that Matthew might be less well accepted
by a new set of neighbors. The father describes family life as having
been significantly defined by their care for Matthew: "We don't do
many things around the house. Things don't get done. We're
spending the better part of our lives, my life, Gertrude's life, taking
care of Matthew. Really. I've been severely criticized by a lot of
people for doing this. Friends of mine. Well-meaning friends. I'm
not sure if they are right or wrong. I really don't know that. I just
feel that Matthew has got to have something. A good life."

Sholanda's father Kevin was more optimistic about the quality
of his family's life, but as in Matthew's family, child-care responsibilities devolved mainly on the mother. Kevin worked hard, dou-
ble shifts on an auto assembly line, to try to support the family. He
became so tired from the heavy work schedule that he broke his
arm in an industrial accident. Meanwhile, his wife Sholanda took
care of young Sholanda. Kevin described her dedication:

> I've got to give it to her. Because you have some people that
> have a child like that . . . that don't want to take that kind of
> responsibility. She was really a champ with that. She was really
> with it. From the time even before Sholanda was even up, she
> was right there. We had all this medicine to give her. I don't
> know what it all was. But Sholanda Senior, she was a whiz.

You would have thought she was a nurse. She had a chart to follow on how much medication the baby was supposed to take. I said, "Sholanda, how do you do it?" And the other three girls she had to take up too. I'm telling you she's a whiz, man. She's a whiz. That woman put a lot of effort in her, man. I ain't telling you no lies, she put a lot of effort in that child, a lot of effort. She didn't halfway sleep, and she was in the room. She suctioned her and she wiped her nose. She would wipe her face and just stay there and talk with her. She would sleep in that room. She'd make a little mat on the floor and she would lay right there.

The fact of the mother as principal care giver is not unusual, not a division of labor made unique by the presence of disability. Mothers do have the principal responsibility for child care in general in this society. Altering this imbalance would presumably require both a reordering of family relations—fathers would need to become more equally responsible for child rearing, and mothers would need equal access to employment outside the home—and the provision of supports such as preschool and school programs, after-school programs, in-home supports such as sitters, and so forth. All the families in this book describe difficulty either in financing sitter or homemaker services or in finding them. The families that do secure sitter services report that it is their own effort, as often as an agency's help, that results in the success.

Integration as Full Participation

More Than an Issue of Access

At the end of Maria's and Felicia's first year in a neighborhood school, the principal informed the Galatis that "it did not work"; the girls would not be invited back. Rose and Dom Galati planned an appeal. They would meet with a district planning and review committee comprising three individuals, one of whom they would be allowed to choose. It was at this point that they heard the rumor of the principal's ultimatum: that he would resign if the board insisted that the Galati girls attend his school. They did not know whether or not to believe the report, but they were not about to give up their struggle to win access for their daughters.

Soon Rose and Dom were summoned to the school board offices, where the assistant director and the superintendent of special services announced, "Well, Mrs. Galati, you've won." Maria and Felicia would continue in the school, and their program would be dictated by the school board, not the principal. The Galatis called off their appeal. But Rose describes the events that followed as a Pyrrhic victory:

> That September was the worst, sending the kids back. I really did struggle with it: "Is this the best place for you to be?" Nobody wanted the kids there. So what did we win? I told the assistant director, "That's fine, but I don't feel that we've won anything." Basically, the kids were in the hallway. My kids were in the hall. The assistants taught them in the hall. They were in the building, they had assistants, the program came from the board, and they could use the toilets. Basically, that was it.

Winning access was clearly not sufficient and not what the Galatis were after. It was a bad year for the girls because they were isolated within the school. It was a bad year for the parents because they were made to feel like outsiders, even villains. "You couldn't communicate with anyone," Rose remembers. "I would approach the school, and you would feel icicles all over the place. That was a bad year."

All along, school integration had been difficult for another reason. Some of the teachers not only lacked experience with integration and with the education of students with severe disabilities but were also vulnerable to the social prejudices that allow people with disabilities to be dehumanized and stereotyped. It was not uncommon, for example, for a child to be spoken about in her presence as if she were not there—even though the speaker could not be certain that the child did not understand. Rose was aware of such insensitivities. They seemed to be part of what "being disabled" meant. In one of the schools in which she was a substitute teacher she saw a sign on a bulletin board calling for "volunteers for TMR class." The term "TMR" stood for "Trainable Mentally Retarded." She wished that people would not use the labels.

At her daughters' own school she encountered another kind of labeling. One teacher kept a chart of Felicia's progress. It was as big as a tabletop and listed in large letters "teeth grinding," "toileting accidents," "drooling," and other behaviors. Rose tried to be positive about it, even though she had her doubts: "It shouldn't have been out in the open. Actually, I thought a lot of it stunk, but I said, 'You know this is a good idea; you're looking at the behaviors, and you're looking at how many times Felicia is doing them, and you're looking at improvement. That's great. But what do you think about putting it in a notebook?'" She knew that the teacher would not make other children's behavior so public; she wanted the same respect for Felicia.

Keeping the Vision

One of the difficult aspects of advocating for her children was her own sense of isolation. It was hard to keep hearing the school board and school staff question her motivations and goal. Rose Galati knew she would not compromise on what she wanted for her children, yet she admits to feeling that maybe she needed to prove to the school board that she was not a bad person and that she *could* be reasonable.

One way to do this would be by agreeing to serve as a substitute teacher in special classes. Each time she did so, however, she became more and more convinced of the correctness of defining integration as participation in typical classrooms rather than merely locating special classes in regular schools: "There is no such thing as the class that's integrated within the school. Its the in-and-out business [students being integrated into particular classes and kept segregated for others], and the kids probably suffer even more." She saw students labeled and talked about as problem children and not belonging anywhere in the school. Consequently, she decided that before she agreed to substitute in any more such classes, she would be nice but firm in telling school principals of her intentions.

"You don't want me," she would offer, "because the only way I will come in there is if you agree to let me integrate the students into regular classes and support them there." Actually, one principal took her up on this offer; she integrated the students.

Rose felt what many parents feel. She had to withhold certain criticisms, knowing that her daughters' school needed some freedom to grow and develop and that if she complained too often, *all* her complaints might be discounted. Also, she wanted to build trust with the teachers and the new principal. She sent muffins to the girls' teachers and did other socially supportive things, but the tension with the school stayed on her mind. Her ambivalence is characterized by the following two accounts.

First, she cautioned a teaching assistant against being too outspokenly critical of the school:

> There was an assistant . . . who came to me. She hated some things. She couldn't stand any kind of rejection of Felicia. She was upset with people talking in front of Felicia. She was upset with teachers complaining about Felicia's presence. She was upset that when the schedule for Felicia had been made up, some teachers refused to let her in their classes at certain periods. But I was at the point where I had done so much work, I just didn't want to hear it. She must have felt we were letting her down, but I said to her, "Look, there is a lot of really good stuff going on for Felicia, and we have to keep working at it. These teachers have just been through muck [because in the controversy with the principal against the parents, the teachers had had to take sides]. We have to go with it.

Second, despite her admonitions to the teaching assistant, Rose did not lessen her own commitment to integration. She could be friendly and supportive without losing her vision of what would be beneficial for Maria and Felicia. After the new principal arrived and the girls were winning greater acceptance, Rose Galati arranged for a specialist in physical therapy to visit the school. The specialist would help design ways for Maria to participate more effectively and to spend more of the day out of her wheelchair. At the planning meeting, one of the school's physical therapists said something that troubled Rose tremendously: "Maria hasn't changed in five years." Rose thought the comment both untrue and unhelpful. "If that's what you truly believe," Rose responded, "then can you tell me how that thought translates into progressive programming for Maria? Because as far as I'm concerned, you've already got a vision for Maria which is nowhere! It doesn't sound to me as if there's room to do something creative." "What else could I say?" Rose asks. "I am a parent, and I wasn't going to sit there and listen to that."

The Galatis and many other families are pioneers. Each time a family achieves integration, the struggle becomes less difficult, and acceptance is more quickly forthcoming. Dominic describes the sense of halting progress:

> There are about forty kids totally integrated in our district right now. And the last report I heard was wonderful stories [from the parents]. All of these are cases where the parents had to fight. But not as much. At least they had to ask [for integration]. No one is going to suggest it to them. No one is going to say, "Oh you can have this." They have to come forward with it [their request] somehow.

Obviously, it would be possible for a school district to adopt inclusion as a universal, systemwide policy in much the same way that districts adopt other policies: for example, achieving racial balance, or having neighborhood schools. The fact that change on this issue usually requires parent pressure probably reflects the degree to which segregation of students with disabilities has become accepted practice. Many districts, including the Galatis', simply had no alternative vision.

The Galatis keep careful track of other families' experiences and with the shifting climate for integration. While their first allegiance is to their own children's education, they know that the best guarantee of their children's participation in regular schools and classrooms throughout their school years lies in broader acceptance of the concept throughout numerous schools. They look forward to Felicia's breaking the exclusion barrier at the high school level in the next year. They welcome the fact that several schools that steadfastly resisted integration in years past have now acquiesced to parental pressure like theirs. At the same time, they are reminded that the school's commitment to integration differs from their own. "Recently," relates Rose, "they asked us, 'How would you feel if we brought a special class into this school?' I said, 'I think it's wrong. I think every child in that class [the special class] belongs in their neighborhood school. I mean I can't stop you if you wanted to do it, but I would fight you if you wanted to do it.' So they thought better of it. They were talking about it, that's all." Although the district did not accept the special class, the fact that it had even entertained the idea stirred Rose and Dom's concern that school officials might still regard Maria and Felicia's presence in typical classes as an isolated experiment, one that might or might not continue.

Ways in Which Schools Can Learn Integration

Trying to fit students with severe disabilities into regular school activities does not always make sense in the particular instance. As one parent admits, it can seem forced, even bizarre: "I watched Johnny Rowe in the middle of a hockey game, flying hockey sticks all over and he is sort of in the middle of these swirling sticks and kids. An aide was with him, being unhelpful. I wasn't sure if that is worth anything, except once or twice so that he can get the idea of what hockey is." Actually, this mother likes her own son Neil to see hockey; she knows he makes the connection between hockey at school and hockey on television. But beyond the benefit to be derived from observing hockey once or twice, "the rest is sort of standing on the sidelines and batting a hockey stick—that I wouldn't call particularly useful." He *can* do exercises along with the other students, his mother points out. Also, he seems to like the general exuberance of other students. When this parent questions a particular event or even a series of events in which her son is not well integrated, she is questioning not the overall validity of his attending the typical school but only the utility or method of certain activities.

Rose Galati shares this parent's view that even though schools are just now learning the how-to of inclusion, that learning process is not bad. "Obviously, if the person [child] wasn't there, there wouldn't be a need for growth and creativity," she argues. "But if the teachers know they have to do it, the more we'll really move forward. And many of the best ideas come from knowing the child." As we saw in the cases of Melvin and Ben, it would have been literally impossible to design school programs without knowing them. Rose Galati envisions teachers brainstorming about how an individual child can participate in school life with other students; she models the process herself:

> I ask myself, what does it mean to be in a regular class? I don't care if she is not doing what the other students are doing. But she shouldn't be having physio [physical therapy] in the back of the class; that belongs in physical education. In math class, doing math kinds of things [she matches hair rollers of the kind that she cleans at the beauty parlor]. But like in geography, what part is she going to do? Well, we decided that Felicia could do something with the display board. She collects the work from the kids and puts it up on the board. She's involved with color. She's watching everything that she's doing constantly.

Achieving "Ordinary Status"

None of the parents interviewed want to have to justify integration into regular classrooms on the basis that their children "learn more there." Rather they argue that integration is a right. Nevertheless, they are quick to point out the learning advantages they do perceive. Rose and Dom see Felicia walking in a more upright posture, establishing eye contact with people (something she had not been doing), developing a few signs such as the one for toileting, being able to walk in groups with other students coming home from school to her neighborhood, and working at the beauty parlor. They note the changes in Maria's fellow students: They have become accustomed to her presence and comfortable with the idea of supporting her. They have learned how to lift her out of her wheelchair, how to eat lunch with her and feed her and give her a drink, how to involve her in what they are experiencing, as when a boy talked with her about what the class was seeing at the museum. They find things about her to admire, such as her ability to move herself on a hammock. One boy from her class regularly calls on the phone and talks to her, even though she cannot speak back.

In contrast, Neil's mother remembers visiting him at a segregated summer school for children labeled retarded. She found it depressing. "I never got over walking in there—kids of all ages. The effect of seeing all those kids together—I don't like the word, but it's deviance is just overpowering." She sighs when she says, "I probably could have gotten over it, but it is nice not to have to."

Though he is still assigned to a special class, Neil has attended his neighborhood schools for all his school years. There he has learned to read, spell, jog, ride a bus, sit next to other students—a whole range of skills. His mother sees the typical high school as both wild and the-right-place-to-be:

> Walk in. Although I am sometimes appalled by the racket and
> the mess and the kids knocking each other over—there is a lot
> of stuff going on over there. It is alive; it is real life. Kids in
> all ranges of dress, all shapes and sizes, all kinds of wonderful
> things and not such wonderful things happening, but it's alive.
> You can't deny that. It is like walking down the street of New
> York City. On occasion it gives you the creeps, but it is really
> alive.

She's not ready to romanticize Neil's life in the world. On the one hand, some kids will say "hi" to him, and he generally does not say anything back or pay any attention whatsoever, "but it is nice that they will make the effort." On the other hand, she also knows that he still may be poked or teased on occasion: "Real integration is yet to come."

Like many parents, Neil's mother counts the events in the child's school life that for her typify the regular status that comes with integration: having a picture in the yearbook, being invited to a friend's house, going to a school dance, getting a report card. Last year Neil's mother sent me a copy of his report card. It looks exactly like those of the other middle school students except that he had the same teacher for all his subjects but physical education (nondisabled students come into his special class during the time they otherwise might attend study hall). His grades were listed as "P" for passing, plus the 75 he received in gym. Teachers' comments included the bland, impersonal, computer-stored phrases: "seems to be trying," "IEP [individualized education plan] goals being achieved," "working to level of ability." Her note to me on this report read, "It doesn't mean much, fitting his progress into this computer format that all students have. But *I LOVE IT!* It's so normal. It's as *BAD* as the report cards for his brother and sister."

Broadening the Definition of What's Allowable

Parents want their children to change in socially acceptable ways, but they also want society to accept them even if their behavior sometimes proves annoying or obnoxious. The question for schools and other social settings is how much such behavior will be tolerated. And if a person acts in very difficult ways, what is the appropriate response? Neil's mother tells of a scene she observed in his middle school, the kind of scene that might cause some people to question school integration as a public policy:

> Wendy is one of the kids with Neil at the middle school. She has a habit of spitting. One day she spit into the hair of a typical student. This student hauled off and screamed at her, and then turned right back to the kid he was talking to and went on with his business. I thought that was just amazing that the student didn't freak out. People don't like to have their hair spit at. He blew up for ten seconds and went back to what he was doing. If another kid had done that, it might be another story. There was no mumbling or further discussion. Wendy is just taken for granted. I think that kind of exposure for the other kids is marvelous.

Behavior like Wendy's challenges the limits of what schoolmates expect to encounter at school and causes them to widen the boundaries of what they can tolerate. At the same time, for Neil and Wendy school integration brings "that unspoken pressure of not being too terribly different and keeping it as under control as you can. It [the pressure] is always in the air."

Not surprisingly, this perspective on how classmates can help improve another student's behavior is almost precisely like what Susan Lehr says of Ben:

> If everybody else in the room is also banging their head on the table and pulling their hair, then that must be the accepted norm. I think no matter how severely retarded or handicapped kids are, they are not dumb. I think they really can perceive themselves in relation to other people around them. Peers exert a lot of pressure on each other. Some of that is positive and some of it is negative. I have heard kids in Ben's class say to him when he is doing something that looks dumb, "That looks dumb." Now he may repeat [the statement] "that looks dumb," but he is also more likely to stop. If kids stay away from him because he is doing something that looks stupid or hurtful, he is aware of that; he doesn't like to be alone. So he will make the effort to try to stop because he wants to be with the kids.

For Sue Lehr as for the other parents, it makes little sense to look for thresholds beyond which schools would be unwilling to accommodate students. Certain behavior might be considered untenable—for example, behavior that could endanger another child—but the school's role, like the parent's, is to discover what a child's behavior means, where it originates, and how to change it when necessary. That process, argue these parents, best occurs in an environment where the expectations are high and where the pressure to find socially acceptable ways of changing behavior is intense.

For a few children, society's notion of acceptable appearance may have to change. A mother reports that when a restaurant waitress stared at her son, she thrust the boy's artificial leg in front of her and said, "Here is his leg, look." Children in this boy's neighborhood play with him and accept him. His artificial leg, colostomy, gastrostomy, and tracheotomy do not keep him from having friends or from being accepted. Yet encounters such as the one in the restaurant are not uncommon.

Parents find ways of coping with their "fish bowl" status. Tasia's mother was asked by her daughter's school principal if Tasia would wear a bonnet during school hours to cover her admittedly disfiguring encephalocoele. Tasia's mother explains that the school officials

> were concerned about parents of the other children [with disabilities] in her room. They thought that these parents were still learning to accept their own children's handicaps, and somehow Tasia was supposed to be making it worse. There was some talk of putting her on the side so that they couldn't see her as well. The principal feels that "Tasia has a right not to have people grossed out by her appearance." That's his philosophy. . . .
>
> My feeling is that yes there are times where maybe people aren't going to interact with Tasia on a regular basis. Like when we go to the store. These are not people who are going to get to know her. So, I agree then. But if people are going to have to interact with Tasia on a regular basis, then there's no other way to get used to her appearance than to see her. There's no use in hiding her.

After consulting with her caseworker, Tasia's mother decided not to comply with the bonnet request. People who would be around Tasia ought to feel comfortable with who she is and what she looks like. She would not cover Tasia or hide her from people who should be accepting of her.

With strangers, she decided to compromise, more for her own and Tasia's benefit than for the public: she would put a bonnet on Tasia when going to the store, because this involved meeting people on a one-time basis. She did not want to have to provide inservice training on attitudes about disabilities every time she and her daughter strolled down the grocery store aisles. Being the parent of a child with a disability meant having to endure a broad range of insensitivities and discrimination, but she decided that since these were so frequent and numerous, to the extent that she had control over them she would decide where, when, and whether to confront them. But she expected people like the school principal to adopt a broader definition of what was acceptable. It is interesting to note that social rejection is present not only in the general population or in so-called mainstream settings but also in "special" disabled-only settings.

Learning to Make It

Sue Lehr believes that it does not make sense to see annoying, abusive, or self-abusive behavior as something set apart from how a person experiences the environment. Consequently, she supports people who look for ways of being and doing that can replace whatever people do that is bothersome or hurtful: "If you teach any person what to do, the things that they shouldn't do will decrease because they will have the right things to do."

Neil's mother too knows that the way he acts relates to how he is treated and what he is feeling. Moreover, Neil's ability to adapt to his world relates directly to his experiences in it. One of the things he learned through school, for example, is how to jog. He has always enjoyed walking fast—he is usually five or ten steps ahead of his dad on walks around the block—but at a jogging track he would not easily concentrate on getting around the track, particularly if there were other things to observe. Through his school program, however, he learned to jog at the local YMCA, alongside businessmen on their lunch hour. He also runs in a local recreation program, at the high school, and at the nearby college fieldhouse. His mother credits experiences like jogging, walking in the halls, being in an ordinary school, having a work-study job in the community, and other social experiences with helping him learn not to run up to other people and grab them or in other ways bother them. He has learned to walk uneventfully through the corridors of his school.

Building Relationships

According to Jeff and Cindy Strully (1985), whose daughter Shawnte[11] developed a close friendship with a schoolmate named Tanya, school integration and the friendships it spawns will protect their daughter from being nothing more than someone's client in her future life. No new-found skills or "competencies" can ensure that their daughter will "make it" in the real world. Rather, they hope for a more supportive society, a place where their daughter can find friendship and concern, perhaps even from people with whom she has been integrated. This seems to be the kind of visibility, acceptance, and even popularity that Rose and Dom Galati see among Felicia and Maria's achievements. Dom describes an incident that he says has become commonplace in the community:

> I work about ten miles away, and last week I went into the local grocery store. There was another man in there who looked familiar. So I asked him, "Don't you run a fish-and-chips store down on Center Street?" He said, "Yeah, and I think I know you too." And I said, "Yeah, I'm one of the teachers who comes in every once in a while." He is a friendly guy. He always jokes around when we go in there. He says, "My teachers, my teachers, how are you?" Anyway, we talked and come to find out he has two children at St. Basil's. I asked, "What grade are they in?" And he said, "Well, the younger one is in Malakovic's class." I said "Oh yeah, does he ever talk about a child who is in a wheelchair?" He said, "Oh, yeah, *Maria*." I said, "Well I'm Maria's father." Well, he couldn't stop talking about Maria.

As Dom told me the story of meeting the fish-and-chips store owner, Rose commented, "It's nice. She's popular. And I can go around and say I'm Maria's mother. And it feels great. It feels great. You can tell from their expressions that they [the people who know Maria and talk about her] feel good about Maria." One set of parents recently told Dom and Rose that every evening at the dinner table their son gives them "an update on what's gone on with

Maria for the day." Rose says that such reports reflect "a lot of good feelings, and that gives you power to keep going."

The concepts of seeing and appreciating the person, lending support, and encouraging participation hardly seem revolutionary. Yet parents speak of them as if they were. And instance after documented instance whereby parents describe both what they want to escape and what they want to embrace suggests a real struggle. This raises a question. What is it about the culture, students classified disabled, and educational policy that makes the personhood, support, and participation of particular students provocative?

CHAPTER IV

The Myth of Clinical Judgment

SPECIAL EDUCATORS usually describe their work as clinical. They treat individuals. If their work is with groups, they nevertheless usually attempt to individualize their "interventions." They are presumed to possess current expert knowledge. And they are expected to exercise professional judgment in each case they handle. They recommend and sometimes have the power to require a *particular* treatment.

At one point or another, the parents interviewed for this book have disputed professional judgment about what their children need and what they can achieve. They have argued with school officials and, in the case of Mary Lou Accetta, with institutional staff. For her daughters Felicia and Maria, Rose Galati is a full-time advocate. She has introduced therapists and teachers to new ideas—about physical therapy, for example, by arranging for a consultant to visit Maria's school, or about "community-based vocational training" by arranging for Felicia to work at a hairdresser's. She and Dom effected a dramatic change in school policy when they won access for their daughters to typical classes in the school. They presented their case to school officials on the basis of what they thought the girls needed: to be with other students; to make friends with students from their neighborhood; to learn from and with nondisabled students; and to be accepted. School administrators and teachers were asked to consider several new concepts in the field—community-based instruction, "partial participation," peer modeling—as well as to shift their judgment regarding where and how the girls might learn and to what end. The Galatis had not begun as experts in severe disabilities, but the better they got to know their own children and the more they came to know the schools, the more they themselves took on the role of expert consultants and advocates.

This chapter attempts to explain why families often feel compelled to become experts on integration. It examines the nature of professional judgment, its authority and meaning for people with disabilities; the chapter analyzes ways in which public policy supports the ideology of professional judgment; it explores the effect on a person's rights of the process of becoming a client and, on a larger scale, considers whether professional judgment achieves what it is expected to achieve. Does it truly treat people individually? Does it reflect the latest expert knowledge?

The material here relies less on parent narratives than on references to educational policies, the demographics of student enrollments and school placements, and educational studies. The data are drawn from the United States, Canada, Australia, and England.

Is Integration a Judgment Call?

Within broadly defined limits, society looks to experts to determine what people with disabilities need. The ordinary citizen's casual comments about people with disabilities reveal how widely disability is equated with client status: "Aren't there special programs for people like this?" "Aren't they better off with their own kind where they can get special treatment and attention?" "Doesn't it take a special kind of person, with special training, to work with them?" Regular schoolteachers often voice a similar concern: "But I don't have the training to work with special education children." It is as if the mark of disability makes a person so different that he or she is assumed to be of another world—the professional's world.

The pervasiveness of this view—disabled-means-different, disabled-as-client—extends to disability policy. Regulations on school placement for example, often summed up in the United States as a search for "the least restrictive alternative," assume that professionals will determine the appropriateness of one approach rather than another. Public Law 94-142 (1975), the Education for All Handicapped Children Act, section 612, requires states to ensure each child a "free appropriate public education" and to establish

> procedures to assure that to the maximum extent *appropriate*, handicapped children, including children in public or private institutions or other care facilities, are educated with children who are not handicapped, and that special classes, separate schooling, or other removal of handicapped children from the regular educational environment occurs only when the nature or severity of the handicap is such that education in regular classes with the use of supplementary aids and services cannot be achieved satisfactorily.

This is civil rights with escape clauses. Students can go to a regular class in a typical school "if appropriate." They can be sent away if the regular class, with support, is deemed ineffective for them to achieve "satisfactorily." As we will see, Canadian policy mimics that of the United States; interestingly, however, the state of Victoria in Australia has rejected the concept of "least restrictive alternative" and the leeway it grants to professionals (Ministerial Review 1984).

In 1982 the U.S. Supreme Court took up its first case under PL 94-142: *Board of Education of the Hendrick Hudson Central School District v. Rowley.* It involved a girl named Amy Rowley who at the time was an elementary school student in the Hendrick Hudson Central School District in New York state. Amy is profoundly deaf. Her parents filed suit against the school district when she was denied the services of a sign language interpreter in her mainstream classes. She was a good student with passing grades. She is an excellent lip reader and thus was able to understand between half and two-thirds of what her teacher and fellow students said in class, but her parents' lawyers framed the case around the notion of equality. They insisted that Amy should enjoy the same educational opportunity as other children. To partake of mainstream education, they argued, she would need interpreter services.

But the court disagreed. Writing for the majority, Justice William H. Rehnquist held that Congress intended the law to guarantee individualized supports to enable a child to "benefit educationally" from instruction. Congress did not intend to impose a standard of *strict* (Rehnquist's term) equality. The decision put neon lights around the law's escape clauses. The court had an opportunity to interpret "free *appropriate* education" to mean access to equal educational opportunity; instead, it chose a lesser standard. Rehnquist spoke of a "basic floor of opportunity" (458 U.S. 201). He carefully ignored the fact that the law itself promises "full educational opportunity." In determining "appropriateness," Rehnquist maintained not only that the court must defer to professional judgment but that it must defer to the state's professionals. In Amy Rowley's case, the state's professionals had determined that she could learn satisfactorily—she had passing grades—in regular classes without interpreter services. The fact that she could understand only half of what was said was immaterial.

In his dissent, Justice Byron White mocked the majority opinion, suggesting that it would apparently satisfy the court's standard of "access to specialized instruction and related services . . . individually designed to provide educational benefit" if a deaf child such as Amy were given a teacher with a loud voice (458 U.S. 215). But Justice Rehnquist warned that "courts must be careful to avoid imposing their view of preferable educational methods upon the states." As he interpreted the act, "the primary responsibility for formulating the education to be accorded a handicapped child, and for choosing the educational method most suitable to the child's needs was left . . . to state and local educational agencies in cooperation with the parents or guardian of the child" (458 U.S. 207–8). In other words the court was unwilling to consider substantive disagreements between parents and state-employed experts so long as the child in question could be determined to be receiving an individualized program of "some" educational benefit and so long as procedures for developing the plan had been followed.

The meaning of this decision for other students with disabilities is obvious. Anyone can see, for example, that Ben and Melvin benefit from their current placements in regular classes, with the support of teaching assistants and teachers who are familiar with severe disabilities. They learn by observing other students. They are developing language. Other students accept them. Yet an unreceptive school board could easily claim that they are not achieving *satisfactorily* or that their program is not really *appropriate*. Their parents could disagree, but unless there had been a procedural error, or clear evidence that groups of students classed as severely disabled are summarily segregated, with no pretense at individualizing placements, the parents' perspective would not prevail over that of the school's experts.

In the American system of special education, any student suspected of having a disability that might interfere with his or her education must be referred for evaluation. Evaluation is seen as leading to placement. The Education for All Handicapped Children Act specifically requires that a team of educators and diagnosticians interpret the assessment results and recommend placement of the student. Further, the law lists a continuum of placement possibilities that the state must guarantee are available: regular classes with supports (resource rooms, consulting teachers, itinerant instruction, teaching assistants or aides); special classes; special schools (that is, separate schools for disabled children only); home instruction; and instruction in hospitals and institutions. Of course, by specifying such a list, the law legitimizes any of these as an appropriate placement; Taylor (1988) says the result of this phenomenon is that students are "caught in the continuum." Thus, professionals can exercise expert judgment within wide boundaries, including placement of individuals in large congregate institutions.

Ironically, PL 94-142 developed out of a recognition that custodial institutions had failed by segregating thousands of children and not educating them. Also, passage of the law reflected Congress's conclusion that the states and the educational community had failed to educate all children, in part because not all children were presumed educable. Most parents and progressive educators saw the law as a way of forcing recalcitrant school districts and officials to educate all children, no matter how severe their disabilities.

Implementation of the "least restrictive alternative" provision has been one of the most controversial aspects of the U.S. law, since it calls for schools to integrate more students with disabilities into the regular public schools than had previously been so served. If the law had merely required school districts to educate all children, without regard to location, the districts could have simply established more programs, many presumably in separate locations. But the "least restrictive" provision gave parents a basis on which to challenge segregation, a reason to hope for integration. Resistance to this agenda by individual school districts has led the federal government to encourage states to establish special procedures to implement and monitor an integration policy. The expectation has been that additional professional review would ensure greater individualization and more appropriate placements. As the U.S. Department of Education reported to Congress (1985, 39):

> Typically, these policies establish a placement process that marshals a wide range of professional expertise and involves several levels of professional review, in order to assure that children are placed in appropriate settings. In some States, these more elaborate placement procedures are used only when the normal IEP [individualized education plan] process has identified a child for whom (1) no appropriate placement is readily available; (2) an out-of-district placement is recommended; or (3) payment for services is contested.

The individual case method is not just a U.S. phenomenon. It characterizes the Canadian, British, Australian, and undoubtedly other nations' experience as well. In the United Kingdom, as in the United States, the rise of special education paralleled the expansion of professionalism in education and psychology and coincided with certain societal demands: for example, the desire to rid schools of students who were perceived as troublesome, unsuccessful, and not fitting. Once the mechanisms of assessment and placement became formalized in policy, professionals' interest in expanding their own spheres of influence may have dramatically hastened the expansion in numbers of special education students.

In England during the early to middle 1900s, school medical officers were empowered to decide whether a child should be labeled as educationally subnormal. The medical officer's status was greater than that of psychologists and was specifically enshrined in the 1944 Education Act (Tomlinson 1981, 49). From 1944 to 1975 the medical officer was *the* expert. By law, the medical officer could assess the child both medically and psychologically (consultation with a psychologist was discretionary) and could make a recommendation to the school administration even without prior contact with the school or family. A government policy circular in 1975 inserted psychologists into the assessment and placement process, between the medical officer—who would henceforth be responsible for a medical exam, though not prohibited from collecting psychological test data—and the final placement decision. The circular encouraged but did not mandate parent participation and consultation (Tomlinson 1981, 55).

Throughout this period, U.K. schools considered special education appropriate for students with mild disabilities (those called "educable retarded" in the United States). Students classified as idiots or imbeciles (also said to have "profound" to "severe" mental retardation, or "custodial" and "trainable" retardation, students who today would be referred to as having severe intellectual disabilities) were excluded from school. They gained admittance in 1975. In 1978, the Warnock Report (DES 1978) recommended a broader-based, team approach (involving psychologists, social workers, therapists, and teachers as well as medical officers) to assessment and placement. Thereafter, educational psychologists were central to the British evaluation process; school social workers filled out a social history form; and, for the first time, parents were required to fill out a form as part of the assessment process, thus guaranteeing them some involvement. Nevertheless, the school would maintain two sets of records for the child: One on educational performance was accessible to the parents; the other including professional perspectives on the family background and other sensitive information, was accessible only to the school professionals (American parents gained full access to school records in 1974). Additional specialists could be consulted as required, including speech and physical therapists, neurologists, occupational therapists; for a student referred for possible special school placement, a minimum of six professionals would be involved. The implicit assumption of the ever more professionalized U.K. system of referral and placement in special education was that expanded professional judgment would yield greater individualization. At the same time, the British team approach like the American, guaranteed that parents were outnumbered and outranked by professionals in the placement process.

Section 2 of the Education Act (1981) in the United Kingdom provided the most far-reaching requirements for local education authorities (LEA) regarding both parental involvement and school integration. In a concise and detailed report titled *Caught in the Act* (Rogers 1986), the Centre for Studies on Integration in Education (CSIE) summarized these responsibilities: first, that LEAs

> should ensure secure appropriate provision for children with
> special educational needs; that they should ensure such chil-
> dren are educated in an ordinary school so long as parents'
> wishes have been taken into account and that this is compati-
> ble with providing what a child needs, ensuring efficient
> education for the other children in the school, and with the ef-
> ficient use of resources; and thirdly that LEAs keep under
> review arrangements for special educational provision. [Rogers
> 1986, 7]

Yet a CSIE survey of the implementation of these requirements revealed unevenness and resistance: only 6 percent of the LEAs had outlined the responsibilities of parents under the Education Act; only 14 percent referred to the act's characterization of parents as partners; only 8 percent provided an explanation of the assessment process; 52 percent failed to mention that parents could request their own evaluation; and 42 percent failed to inform parents of their right to appeal an LEA decision.

Some LEAs provided concise information to parents in a simple, appealing form, but most did not. LEA publications that included pictures of children rarely portrayed scenes of students in integrated settings. Some LEAs distanced themselves from the law with such language as "this booklet contains information which . . . [we] are required to publish in connection with special education provision." The same booklet tells parents, "It is recognized that the procedures explained in this booklet may seem rather complicated. However, as the Authority is legally required to carry out these procedures it is difficult to further simplify them." Another undoubtedly left many parents wondering what is being communicated: "The LEA follows the regulations of the DES [Department of Education and Science] for assessing the needs of children who appear to require any form of special education." One local educational authority seemed uncomfortable with the law and regulations concerning parents-as-partners: "The Act gives the Authority the power to require the co-operation of parents . . . but also gives parents the right to be consulted at all stages"—hardly a welcoming invitation to collaboration. Other LEAs undermined the act's new preference for integration: "If it is what you want, the [LEA] . . . will try to arrange for your child to be educated in an ordinary school. This can only be done, however, if his educational needs can be fully met in an ordinary school, if the education of other children in the school is not likely to be adversely affected and if the cost of making the necessary arrangements in the ordinary school is not too high." Some less reluctant authorities, however, did show themselves more open to integration, using such phrases as "in most cases," "as far as (or wherever) possible," and "all reasonable efforts are made" (Rogers 1986, 5–8).

Individualization is the cornerstone of the American system established before the appearance of the Warnock Report. The U.S. special education law mandates assessment beyond standardized assessments alone. It requires tests individually tailored to a child's suspected needs, tests in the native language of the child, tests that are valid for the purpose used, and assessment in all areas related to a child's suspected disability, including health, vision, hearing, social and emotional status, general intelligence, academic performance, communicative status, and motor (physical movement) abilities. Moreover, the assessment must be made by "a multidisciplinary team or group of persons, including at least one teacher or other specialist with knowledge in the area of suspected disability" (PL 94-142, 20 U.S.C. 1412[5][C]). Similarly, placement decisions must be made by a group of people knowledgeable about the evaluation data and placement options. Parents must be informed of and may object to decisions to perform an assessment or make a placement, but they are participants in neither procedure except as informants.

The Canadian situation closely parallels the American and British school officials' autonomy to determine the appropriateness of an educational program. Until 1985, Canada lacked a "rights" provision that would ensure access to education. A few Canadian courts supported education for all children, but they were unwilling to question or judge school boards on the nature and quality of instruction (e.g., *Carriere v. Lamond Board of Education* 1978, and *Bales v. Board of School Trustees* 1984). In 1982, however, Canada adopted a new constitution that included a "Charter of Rights and Freedoms." Section 15 of the charter, incorporating language similar to that of the U.S. Constitution's 14th Amendment, became effective in 1985: "Every individual is equal before and under the law and has the right to the equal protection and equal benefit of the law without discrimination based on race, national or ethnic origin, colour, religion, sex, age or mental or physical disability."

This provision has provided the basis for legal challenges to segregated special schools; at the same time, however, educators have been quick to claim their prerogative in interpreting the meaning of equality vis-à-vis appropriate educational practice for students with disabilities. Moreover, another provision of the charter allows individual provinces to argue that certain laws must operate outside the reach of the charter's equal protection provision. For these and other reasons, the practices of individual school boards vary significantly. Some boards operate special schools, and others do not. Some integrate students with severe disabilities in classes with students who have no disabilities, but most do not.

In an effort to limit professional prerogative in the placement of students, the Education Ministry of Victoria, Australia, adopted a policy in 1984 of guaranteeing the right of any child to attend his or her local school. Joan Reidy, then president of the State School Parent Organization and a member of the panel that wrote the report issued by the Ministerial Review of Educational Services for the Disabled (1984), had traveled to the United States several years earlier to observe the effects of PL 94-142 on school integration, and had noted the enormous disparities between school districts and states in their implementation of the integration provision. Consequently, she advocated an unequivocal policy that would support the right of a child to attend his or her local school.

The review panel was mindful that the American and British special education reforms, by leaving in-tact or expanding the labeling system and various tests of access as preconditions for any specialized support or service and for integration itself, had fostered a continuance of segregation. Hence, the panel agreed on a simple declaration for integration: "Every child has a right to be educated in a regular school." Its report, *Integration in Victorian Education*, specifically rejects the "notions of 'least restrictive environment' and 'most appropriate setting'" on the grounds that these terms give too much power to professionals. By making integration a right, the report attempts "to equalize the relationship between parents and service providers, including professionals." It defines integration as "a process of increasing the participation of children with impairments and disabilities in the education programs and social life of regular schools in which their peers without disabilities participate" and "a process of maintaining . . . participation." Elaborating far beyond the U.S. model, it further defines this process of increasing participation as "getting into the regular classroom those children who are presently segregated from it" (Ministerial Review 1984, 6–7).

Unlike the United States, the United Kingdom, and Canada, Victoria policy expressly excludes psychologists or other professionals from determining placement:

> Educational service providers should focus on changing the nature of the educational environment [especially that of the regular school] in order to reduce the educationally handicapping consequences which may otherwise follow from certain impairments and disabilities. The prime focus . . . is therefore on educational services and not a clinical focus on any deficit a child may be deemed to have. The Review . . . believes that the terms ascertainment [assessment and classification] and placement are inappropriate in a context where the prime con-

cern in enacting a policy of integration is with changing the
educational setting in order to reduce any educational handicaps a child may encounter in that setting. [Ministerial
Review 1984, 8]

The Victorian report further rejects the term "special needs" because of its association with the "deficit model" (that is, seeing the
problem as within the child rather than in a nonadapting school or
school system) and because it is "noncontained" (that is, such a
term can be applied to nearly anyone and therefore is meaningless
as a tool for education planning). The Victorians note with some
shock the claim of the Warnock Report (DES 1978) that one in
five children will require some kind of special educational provision
in their school careers (Ministerial Review 1984, 8). With the
abandonment of psychological assessments as a prerequisite to
placement, parents can simply come to the local school and be as-
sured of their children's access. It is then left to "Enrollment and
Support Groups" comprising both professionals (principal, teacher,
psychologist) and the parents (identified as full participants) to design an appropriate program. In general, however, parents still find
themselves outnumbered in this planning process. Thus, their influence depends mainly on their own advocacy, their alliances with
parent support groups, the history of integration in their particular
community, and, as in the past, on the disposition of the professionals they encounter.

     Education laws and policies in Canada, the United States, the
United Kingdom, and Victoria, Australia, articulate a presumption
that students with disabilities benefit by going to school with students who do not have disabilities. In the United States and in
Victoria particularly, this aspect of educational policy has a distinct
rights tone, yet the rights declarations do nothing to force an end
to separate schooling. In none of these countries has there been a
systematic review of separate schooling; none has outlawed or
withdrawn funding from separate special schools. Rather, it is assumed that parents will accomplish what politicians and government officials have found too politically frightening. Parents are
expected to change the landscape of educational settings slowly

through their child-by-child requests for access to regular schools and classes. In other words, parents are asked to transform century-old patterns of segregation through individual case advocacy on behalf of their sons and daughters, even if it means challenging school districts, school boards, and their corporate attorneys. And if the parents lose, they can make appeals.

On this matter, U.S. Supreme Court Justice Rehnquist was as sympathetic as Marie Antoinette telling the breadless peasants to eat cake: "As this very case demonstrates [*Board of Education v. Rowley* 1982] parents and guardians will not lack ardor in seeking to ensure that handicapped children receive all of the benefits to which they are entitled by the Act" (458 U.S. 209). It is noteworthy that this first PL 94-142 case to reach the Supreme Court did not do so until seven years after the law passed Congress. Initially, Amy Rowley's parents had taken their appeal to a hearing officer, as mandated under the federal law. They lost: the hearing officer decided in favor of the school officials. Next, they appealed their case to New York State's Commissioner of Education. Again, they lost: the commissioner affirmed the hearing officer's decision. Next, they took their case to a U.S. District Court. Here, for the first time, they won: the judge found that although Amy had made friends and was progressing well, even better than average, she could not understand much of what was said in class; without an interpreter she could not achieve to her potential. Now, the school district appealed to a federal Appellate Court. Again, Amy's parents won. Again, the school district appealed, this time to the U.S. Supreme Court. Finally, Amy lost. Justice Rehnquist's assurances notwithstanding, we cannot help wondering how many parents would have the "ardor" for such struggle.

Lost Rights

In the United States the Rehabilitation Act of 1973 includes an anti-discrimination clause (section 504) and an affirmative action in hiring clause (section 503). Similarly, the disabilities assistance legislation passed two years later includes a bill of rights (Develop-

mentally Disabled Assistance and Bill of Rights Act 1975). That act
of Congress followed on the heels of a national furor over exposés
of horrid institutional conditions, including excessive deaths by
pneumonia; epidemics of scabies, hepatitis, and other diseases; reports of rampant physical abuse and sexual assaults; unclothed in-
mates, massive overmedication with crippling side effects,
institutional overcrowding, and an absence of therapeutic programs
(Blatt 1970 and 1973; Kugel and Wolfensberger 1969; Rivera
1972). Like the education rights legislation of the same year, the
Developmentally Disabled Assistance and Bill of Rights Act, section 6010, sought to ensure *appropriate* treatment in the "least restrictive setting":

> Persons with developmental disabilities have a right to appro-
> priate treatment, services and habilitation for such disabilities.
>   The treatment, services, and habilitation for a person with
> developmental disabilities should be designed to maximize the
> developmental potential of the person and should be provided
> in the setting that is least restrictive of the person's liberty.

This law was similar to the education law in another way as well. It
left open the matter of who should decide the meanings of "appropriate" and "least restrictive" and on what basis.

When the Supreme Court ruled in *Youngberg v. Romeo* (1982),
which relied heavily on this act, the majority decision followed the
reasoning in *Rowley*. The case concerned Nicholas Romeo, a man
classified as having profound retardation:

> He cannot talk and lacks the most basic self-care skills. Until
> he was 26 . . . [he] lived with his parents in Philadelphia. But
> after the death of his father in May 1974, his mother was un-
> able to care for him. Within two weeks of the father's death . . .
> [his] mother sought his temporary admission to a nearby
> Pennsylvania hospital. Shortly thereafter, she asked [to have
> him] admit[ted] to a state facility on a permanent basis. [457
> U.S. 307]

Shortly after Nicholas entered the institution, his mother began to
complain about his treatment. Her lawsuit alleged that Nicholas
had been injured sixty-three times in two years, including having

his arm broken. She accused the institution of physically restraining her son over prolonged periods of time. Among other things, the case sought for Nicholas the provision of treatment or activity programs, the removal of restraints, and the assurance of physical safety.

Writing for the majority, Justice Lewis Powell accepted the standard that had been adopted by the appeals court's Chief Judge Seitz, that "the constitution only requires that the courts make certain that professional judgment in fact was exercised. It is not appropriate for the courts to specify which of several professionally acceptable choices should have been made" (457 U.S. 321). Within certain broad, constitutionally protected limits—as in *Rowley*—the Supreme Court vested authority not only in professional judgment but in the judgment of the state's experts; despite vastly different circumstances—Amy Rowley was doing well, and Nicholas Romeo was not—this decision was *Rowley*'s twin:

> We agree that respondent [Nicholas Romeo] is entitled to minimally adequate training [the Court noted that the state may not incarcerate someone for "care and protection" without paying some heed to the notion of care]. In this case the minimally adequate training required by the Constitution is such training as may be reasonable in light of . . . [Romeo's] liberty interests in safety and freedom from unreasonable restraints. In determining what is "reasonable"—in this and in any case presenting a claim for training by a State—we emphasize that courts must show deference to the judgment exercised by a qualified professional. . . . Decisions made by the appropriate professional are entitled to a presumption of correctness. Such a presumption is necessary to enable institutions of this type—often, unfortunately, overcrowded and understaffed—to continue to function. . . . The administrators and particularly professional personnel, should not be required to make each decision in the shadow of an action for damages. [457 U.S. 322, 324–25)

Predictably then, if parents or people with disabilities disagree with a state's experts, the courts will nearly always defer to the official experts. The assumption is that their professional judgment qualifies them to evaluate the rights a person has (what is appropriate, what is least restrictive) in particular circumstances *and* that since the court is not expert itself in such matters, it must not impose its views; it must accept the state's words as its own.

The courts and the public would never abrogate the rights of nondisabled people in the same way. School officials could not segregate students on the basis of their height or hair color. The state cannot institutionalize a nondisabled child or adult unless he or she has been represented by an attorney and been found delinquent. Yet the child classified as disabled has no such protection, not even a right to legal representation in commitment proceedings.

Naturally, some parents ask: Is it right for the state's experts to have sole authority to determine what is "appropriate" for people with disabilities? Should courts and society defer to state experts to decide whether to institutionalize a child, to segregate students with disabilities into separate schools, or to decide whether a child shall be physically restrained or even punished in the name of treatment? We might ask other questions. Should any child or, for that matter, any adult be institutionalized for reasons of disability? Should school districts separate any students from regular schools and classes? In defending themselves against such forced segregation, should people with disabilities and their own experts have less authority than state experts?

A father in Canada who has weathered several administrative appeals en route to winning the opportunity for his daughter with severe disabilities to attend regular high school classes conveys the frustration and disillusionment of many parents with due process procedures:

> We went through the appeals process, which was unsuccessful. It's an appeal process that is an illusion. School boards still have all the power, but it makes parents feel they have a chance of overturning something. Once in a hundred cases that happens. In most cases, [the outcome] is entirely predictable. The [appeals] board includes the superintendent of the school board. Another is a representative of an association that is selected by the parents. The third one is the chairperson

chosen by the school board. Typically they select a superintendent or someone in a very high position from another school
board. So the school board chooses two of the three people
who sit on it. The weird thing is, even if the parents win, the
decision goes to the [school] board trustees [comparable to
U.S. school board members] which then decide whether or
not to comply. An appeal is more formal, [parents] have to
hire a lawyer, and it all takes a long time.

Under such ground rules, this father feels powerless. The likelihood
that school superintendents and officials will disagree with one another is slim.

Another parent from the same district talks about the pressure
on school experts to go along with prevailing policy: "None of the
people on the school board have acknowledged support for our
position [for regular-class integration]. We have met people who
have been quite sympathetic privately. But publicly, they feel
threatened. Very obviously, they are *not* to support anything that
has anything to do with integration. They can't go public." This
picture of educators afraid to speak their minds raises serious questions about the fairness of disability policy founded on professional
judgment as well as the ability of experts to exercise judgment. Are
they able to? If their role is diminished to rationalizing and legit-
imizing state actions that might otherwise seem discriminatory,
they are merely pawns in a system that deprives people with disabilities of the right to participate in community life.

Not a Judgment at All

Sandy Sellars is thirteen years old. Her parents describe her as being like other students her age: she enjoys doing her work on a
computer, attending school dances, and working on the school
newspaper. Unlike many of her schoolmates, Sandy has Down
syndrome.

She attends a Green Gable, California, middle school one mile
from her house. She has been in nonsegregated schools since kin-

dergarten: "She's always appreciated being with the other kids," her mother says. Sandy attends a typical art class, goes to recess and the cafeteria with nondisabled students. Last year at a PTA-sponsored summer program she was with nondisabled students in every activity. Her parents are currently advocating that Sandy be placed in regular academic classes with nondisabled students. If this means that she will sometimes encounter a snicker or negative comment, her mother reasons that she can learn from it: "Sandy needs to develop strategies to deal with that, no matter how weird other kids can be sometimes."

The irony is that if Sandy lived one mile east, in the Lebanon Unified School District, she would probably attend a separate school for disabled students only. At the very least her parents would have to advocate for a regular school placement, and even if they won, the placement would not likely be in her neighborhood school. Lebanon has a few special education classrooms in regular schools, but the district operates eighteen segregated schools for disabled students only. In such a system, students with severe or moderate disabilities who *do* attend regular schools can expect to be shuttled from one school to another, depending on where the special program is located. In other words, they do not get to go to school with nondisabled students from their own neighborhoods.

The national picture of student placements reflects similarly extreme variations. Although 92 percent of all students labeled handicapped attend regular classes, special classes, resource classes, or some combination of these in regular schools, this figure is deceiving. For example, students classified as learning-disabled and speech-impaired together account for 67 percent of all students labeled handicapped, but they are segregated less than 2 percent of the time. Once they are taken out of the statistics, the degree of segregation for students with other types of disabilities rises dramatically.

A number of states segregate large numbers of certain disability groups into separate special schools. Among students labeled retarded, the rate of segregation can be high—Delaware and the District of Columbia 37 percent each, Maryland 40 percent, Louisiana 23 percent, New York 30 percent, Nevada 29 percent, New Jersey

23 percent, and Texas 20 percent—yet remarkably, thirteen states segregate less than 3 percent of students classified as retarded. In New York state, 10,793 students (26 percent) labeled emotionally disturbed are segregated. Other states that segregate substantial numbers of students labeled emotionally disturbed include California (21 percent), Delaware (25 percent), Illinois (32 percent), Kentucky (38 percent), Maryland (61 percent), Minnesota (33 percent), New Jersey (25 percent), Ohio (49 percent), and Pennsylvania (23 percent), yet again, a number of states segregated almost none of their students labeled emotionally disturbed. Those classified as multihandicapped are the most often segregated—for example, Maryland and Texas segregate 80 percent of this group, New York 61 percent—but in contrast, Massachusetts reported that it segregated less than 5 percent of the same group (U.S. Department of Education 1985, 242–45).

Taking all categories of disability, the states with the lowest rate of segregation overall are ten times less likely to segregate any labeled students than are the states that segregate the most (Danielson and Bellamy 1989). States that have an average level of segregation are five times more likely to segregate a student than are those that segregate the fewest.

Similar patterns exist outside the United States. In Canada, for example, some school districts in New Brunswick segregate no students, yet other districts operate special schools. In Ontario, several publicly funded Catholic school boards educate students with severe disabilities in regular classes, while their counterpart regular school boards in the same regions segregate all such students.

Comparisons within the United States are made more difficult by the states' inconsistency in classifying students as disabled or as having particular disabilities. More than 50 percent of all the students labeled handicapped in Alaska and California are identified as learning-disabled, but less than one-third of the students with handicaps in Wisconsin and South Carolina have that designation. A student labeled handicapped is more than six times as likely to be classified emotionally disturbed in New York state than in California. A student labeled handicapped in Ohio is 2.5 times more likely to be classified as mentally retarded than a student in Wisconsin or

Texas (U.S. Department of Education 1988). There is little agreement on who has particular disabilities. A group of researchers who focused on the classification of learning disability found no clear difference between students who are labeled and served separately and those who are unlabeled and simply regarded as low achievers in the regular classes (Ysseldyke et al. 1982). The mild disability categories comprise more boys than girls and more minority than nonminority students. But here too, variations abound. Minorities are disproportionately represented in the larger school districts and in southern school districts. Predominantly minority schools have less disproportion than schools with lower (say, 30 percent) minority enrollment (Heller, Holtzman, and Messick 1982, 8–10).

What are we to conclude from these differences? Certain nonclinical factors have been identified as influencing placement practices and, therefore, professional judgment. One obvious explanation is that funding policies influence the nature of services or labeling. If a state contributes 100 percent of the funds for an institutional or residential school placement, compared with only a proportion of the cost of educating a student in a local school, that school will have an incentive to exclude students and send them to the state institution. Similarly, the proportion of students in separate private schools increases when states provide more favorable funding to these settings than to local schools (Blatt 1972). Among the states having high levels of segregated placements of students with moderate and severe retardation, emotional disturbance, and multiple disabilities are those that have provided state funding for the construction of regional separate schools: Ohio, New York, Illinois, New Jersey, Missouri. Further, certain types of state funding to individual school districts can influence the percentage of students identified and the degree to which students are educated in regular or special classes and the proportional representation of minorities in those settings (Magnetti 1982).

Other nonclinical factors believed to influence the rate of placement of students in separate schools include a past practice of segregating students, the prior existence of separate schools, lack of experience with regular school and classroom placement of students with severe disabilities, parent advocacy, and regulatory limitations on out-of-school and out-of-district placement.

What Is the Basis for Judgment?

Science will not tell society what to do with people who have disabilities—for two reasons. First, some assessments cannot be "proved," at least not in the same sense that a mathematical or physical principal can be proved. For example, the concept of a right to education for all children assumes that all children can learn, but that assumption is not amenable to proof. While educators might debate whether a child with, for example, anencephaly can learn, most agree that we should act on the belief that all children can learn. Teachers must assume that if a child does not show evidence of learning, the problem resides not in the child but in the teacher's inability to discover an effective teaching strategy. To do otherwise is to risk consigning some children to custodialism and depriving them of learning.

The second reason is that science is not policy. Science can provide information to help society make decisions about what to do—for example, by studying the effects of different teaching strategies—but answers to the questions that society is most concerned with usually elude research.

For years educators have studied and debated the pros and cons of school organization and the best strategies for students with severe disabilities. Such research is plagued by questions about what constitutes a "regular school" or a "special school," as well as how to control for differences in curricula. Legal requirements for placing individual students according to their unique needs precludes the creation of traditional controlled studies; although it would be possible to match student characteristics in special and regular schools, researchers would have to determine whether differences arising between these schools were attributable in part to the research itself. For these and other reasons, studies related to the effects of typical and special schooling tend to address narrower questions.

Literature that reviews the relative efficacy of special schools or classes and regular schools or classes notes the difficulties of controlling for variables other than integration and segregation (Blatt 1977). Given these problems, however, the literature does *not* provide evidence that segregated schools facilitate learning better than regular schools. When they attend regular classes and regular schools, students with disabilities have broader opportunities to observe the behavior of and interact with nondisabled students, in academic as well as social situations (Biklen 1985; Brinker and Thorpe 1984; Knoblock 1982). Integration breeds acceptance among students. More physical integration leads to greater acceptance by nondisabled students of students classified as disabled (Towfighy-Hooshyar and Zingle 1984). Planned or structured interaction produces even greater tolerance, acceptance, and interaction than does mere proximity (Biklen 1985; Biklen, Corrigan, and Quick 1989; Knoblock 1982; and Voeltz 1982). Also, autobiographical accounts by students who have been integrated reveal that they often view themselves as ordinary students: that is, not different from students who are not labeled (see, Biklen, Corrigan, and Quick 1989; Kaye 1981). One study found that when interaction between students with and without disabilities was systematically supported, the increased student-to-student interaction correlated with greater success by the labeled students on their IEP goals (Brinker and Thorpe 1984). In other words, although interaction is often thought to be a side benefit of integration, it may have a crucial role in facilitating improved academic performance. This finding should not be surprising; essentially, it says that students will perform well when they feel accepted and valued.

Integrated schooling provides expanded options for informal learning. Also, when schools help students learn social skills, academic knowledge, and work skills incidentally or in informal situations rather than in highly structured, laboratory-like situations, these skills and knowledge may be easier to recall and use in future social situations (see, e.g., Brown, Ford et al. 1983; Brown, Nisbet et al. 1983; Brown, Shiraga et al. 1986; Coon, Vogelsberg, and Williams 1981; Halle 1982; Liberty, Haring, and Martin 1981).

Follow-up studies of how students fare when they graduate suggest the benefit of early integrated schooling (Brown, Shiraga et al. 1986; Wehman et al. 1982; Wilcox and Bellamy 1982): integration correlates with successful job placement and job retention. In other words, integration in school is a predictor of integration in later life. In part, integrated schooling may cause students and teachers alike to expect that continued integration is possible. Educators have been found to be more optimistic about the future of students they see engaged in useful (and more integrated) activities than that of students doing make-work (in more segregated situations) (Bates et al. 1984). Success in later life may also be related to the greater likelihood that the individual education plans of students in regular schools will reflect research-based "best practices" than will the IEPs of students in schools for disabled students only (Hunt, Goetz, and Anderson 1986).

A final compelling research finding concerns feasibility. Certain regular schools and school districts have demonstrated that they can provide effective educational programs to even the most severely disabled students (Forest 1987; Taylor and Ferguson 1985). This leads us to ask, is it not therefore possible to do so also in other schools and districts?

Obviously, such research findings answer certain questions but raise others. If students seem to learn to accept one another more when they are encouraged to interact, what form does that encouragement take? If students with disabilities encounter prejudice ("handicapism"), should this cause us to question integration? Or attack the prejudice? These questions suggest the problem of trying to conceptualize and evaluate education from a scientific perspective. Scientific investigation can provide information; it cannot tell society how to behave, who to value, or where its future lies.

CHAPTER V

Two Students, One Myth

STATED SIMPLY, the myth of clinical judgment means that parents, educators, and the public at large are encouraged to think that decisions about where and how to educate students with disabilities are made primarily or even solely on the basis of professional judgment—when in fact other, nonclinical factors figure largely in such decisions. This chapter further substantiates the contradiction between myth and reality by looking at how two families have experienced educational decision-making. Their stories center on recognizing and combatting the myth of clinical judgment. In resisting mechanistic treatment, the families found themselves becoming change agents and concluding that their children's future depends on clinical know-how *and* political advocacy.

Education through Rejection

Linda Till was working for the Ontario Association for Community Living (OACL), providing infant stimulation to children with intellectual disabilities in nursing homes, when she met a four-year-old child named Becky who weighed only thirteen pounds. Institutionalized from birth, Becky has mixed, athetoid cerebral palsy. At that first meeting her body was curled up, her muscles were atrophied, and she was unsmiling. When told that Becky did not smile, Linda responded, "Well, she has to have something to smile about." Becky lived in a small room with five other children in a nursing home that housed thirty-three children.

Five months after it began at the institution, the infant stimulation project was terminated. "We were too threatening," Linda recalls. But Becky had made a connection with Linda Till. Linda had begun to take her home for weekends, and when it became increasingly difficult to return her to the nursing home, Linda and her husband, King, decided to adopt the child.

Meanwhile, Linda began to direct a project for the OACL with a specific focus on advocacy for people with developmental handicaps who were living in Ontario nursing homes. "They hired me to 'tackle' the issues of nursing home conditions," she said. "The way I would do it is by trying to close these places down." (In fact, by June 1990 all *had* closed.) Linda Till's association with Becky had begun out of her conflict with nursing home officials over the care of children like Becky; this conflict would soon broaden to other areas of human services, particularly the schools.

Catherine Woronko was not disabled at birth, but at five months she had a severe reaction to an inoculation against childhood diseases. Doctors told her parents that she had suffered severe brain damage, and she spent most of the next seven months in the hospital, heavily sedated.

In describing Catherine, her father talks as much about what she *can* do as about her deficits:

> She learned to walk when she was six or seven years old. Before that she would walk on her knees. We had a hard time getting her to walk on her feet. She doesn't speak. We attempt to communicate with signs. She has a sign for drink, a sign for music, and a sign for asking to go to the washroom [toilet]. We have not succeeded in having her learn any other signs. I try to get her to communicate with picture cards. The difficulty there is to get her to look at them. She now laughs fairly well. She still hasn't learned to run. That doesn't particularly concern us. She can walk fairly long distances. She also behaves in a strange way with her vision. It is very hard to get eye contact with her. She doesn't tend to focus too much on things. Except there definitely are times when she is interested in food or something and she will focus. When she is going

down stairs, walking on a sidewalk, or approaching a curb, she doesn't look at it; she feels it with her feet. I suspect there is some complicated equivalent of a learning disability. But exactly what it is we may never know. It's curious.

The Woronkos and the Tills live in the same school district just outside of Toronto, Ontario. Although Catherine Woronko was ready to enter public school in the 1970s, several years earlier than Becky, the families' experiences with access were fairly similar. Linda Till sees the workings of placement as stereotyped and bureaucratic:

> Our board's process for dealing with kids with labels is equivalent to: "Identify the label. The label dictates the placement and program absolutely." There is no option for an individual approach. Despite the language of the law . . . the board's approach is . . . multihandicapped kids in a multihandicapped placement, . . . trainable mentally retarded kids in a trainable class, . . . language-limited kids in a language class.

According to Linda, families hardly have time to digest the placement marching orders, let alone formulate questions or present their own thoughts; on the average, the individual planning conference takes ten minutes. Having served at a number of these as a parent advocate, Linda describes the meeting as more "announcement" than "conference." "They have the report all written out for parents: 'Okay, this is the identification. This is the placement. Sign.'"

The school board wanted to send Becky to a multihandicapped class in which all the other students were nonverbal. But when the Tills secured outside funding for an aide's services, Becky was allowed into a special education class that included students, who, though still labeled multihandicapped, "were really capable and could talk and could walk." Linda believes that no students need to be removed from typical classes or placed in special ones: "I don't understand how anyone thinks those kids should be segregated. Really, they were capable." This placement did give Becky an opportunity to hear normal language and to participate in some typical classes for parts of her school day; nevertheless, Linda Till resented the idea that Becky should have to "buy" her way into it—it was like being asked to bring one's own dish to a meal that for everyone else was catered. When the grant for the aide service expired, so did the school board's magnanimity. Becky was moved to another special class, one that already had extra aides but not classmates who could talk. The Tills argued that "individualization" should mean creating program supports where a child can benefit most. Becky could learn to read and to do math if someone would teach her. And she could learn from other students. The board was not persuaded.

The Woronkos had a similar experience, although it was several years before they sought integration for Catherine. For the first six years of her schooling, they avoided sending their daughter to the board's special school, which they felt was understaffed, by enrolling her in a special campus school at a local college. This was a segregated program, in Stan Woronko's words, it was "richly resourced." The school's curriculum included such things as learning to eat with a spoon, identification of objects, toileting, and exercises or activities that encouraged students to make eye contact with other people, to focus on objects, and to play games.

When Catherine turned twelve, however, she was no longer eligible for the campus program and was placed in the board's separate school. The Woronkos felt discouraged by what they observed there and stymied by the lack of other options; for Catherine Woronko, as for Becky Till, the promise of an individualized program seemed hollow. Catherine's behavior deteriorated. She would sit and chew on objects, literally anything near her. She whined a great deal. Stan Woronko remembers hearing from social workers and others that children at the school were often left to rock in a corner, bored and uninvolved. As he recalls, he did not know what precisely was wrong, but he began to demand that the school identify specific goals for Catherine and evaluate her progress toward them. He complained that Catherine's school day was a half-hour shorter than it would be in a regular school. But none of this program monitoring seemed to improve Catherine's situation or disposition: "It was just getting more and more frustrating. We weren't getting anywhere."

Becky's prospects were little better than Catherine Woronko's;

she too seemed to be following a special education placement template. The special class to which she was assigned was in a regular school, but in another town. The Tills felt worried about Becky's education and future and frustrated that the school board seemed to regard her as just one more "case" to place:

> That class happens to be filled with a number of kids who have significant disabilities, multiple, severe [disabilities]. We have been saying all along that the bottom line, the simplest thing to understand, is that she needs to be around other kids who can talk. She needs to be around kids who can walk and who can come up to her and initiate interaction, because obviously she cannot do that to them. She benefits from that. She's motivated by that. She needs that. They can't be duplicated in an environment where the other children can't talk and even with assistance can't walk. The teacher in the class was heard by another parent to have said that "two of the kids in the class were, quote, vegetables."

Besides feeling that their daughters had been pigeonholed, the Woronkos and Tills found them unwanted: these schools were not welcoming their children. They were not recognizing their virtues, their strengths, their unique talents. Linda Till remembers being told that Becky had been taken out of a school assembly because she became excited and laughed, that Becky's physical presence was disruptive to the other students. In other words, she was thoroughly segregated, a true outsider.

The realization that Catherine was similarly an outsider and that her exclusion was at the heart of his frustration came more slowly for Stan Woronko. Monitoring her program from a distance gave him a feeling of doing *something*, however ineffective, but not until he attended a meeting at which the principal of a Catholic school in Hamilton, Ontario, spoke of school integration did he begin to grasp the depth of Catherine's exclusion: "The principal showed slides of children being integrated. I was very moved by how receptive they were, and I wished that my daughter could go to a school like that." It was the receptive attitude that impressed him, even more than the integration itself. His embrace of the integration philosophy would come later.

Mechanisms

In addition to being placed in ready-made, not individualized, school situations, Becky and Catherine also encounter programmatic and relational templates. Although her parents believe that Becky understands nearly all of what she hears and sees—though not perhaps words or situations that are new to her—the world tends to define her in more limiting ways. The school board classifies and perceives her as multihandicapped, severely intellectually disabled, and totally dependent. It took the Tills two and a half years to convince school officials that Becky needed a desk and chair at school, that she could learn to sit at a desk, and that she should not spend the entire day in her wheelchair. The wheelchair actually limited her ability to do academic work in the classroom. A teacher could not easily spread books out in front of her while she was in the chair, for example. At home she had a chair precisely as high as the length of her legs from the knees down, so that when she sat, her feet rested on the floor; a desk with a slightly tilted top was set at a proportionate height. With this arrangement Becky learned to sit up, even though "this is a kid" her mother points out, "who goes into all kinds of extension thrusts and reflexes and stuff that pull her all over the place. So she had to learn how not to do that. You learn that you *better* learn that, because if you don't, you hit your head on the back of the chair or you fall off the side." The school therapist admitted to being skeptical that Becky could sit at a desk. But when she finally visited the Tills' home and saw for herself that Becky could indeed sit, she exclaimed, "My God, you're right," and immediately ordered a similar desk and chair for the school. It arrived just two weeks before the end of the session. But Becky has not been back to school since then because the board wants to segregate her in a multihandicapped class that her parents reject as anti-educational.

It is difficult to escape presumptions about what a person can or cannot do, or what is important or unimportant to that person. At one time or another, nearly everyone will make some presumptions about Becky and Catherine or anyone with a severe disability, particularly if the disability is one that hinders communication. Linda Till recalls attending a conference in which she, her husband, and Becky were to appear on a panel together. The audience was interested in hearing their perspective on community living, family support, and such matters. Linda and King discussed the presentation with Becky. They decided with Becky that she would talk about the "best part of living in a family," which she says is being hugged. Her parents set her up with her yes/no voice box connected to head switches: when she tilts her head to one side, the voice box says "Yes"; the other way, it says "No." They went over the questions in advance and Becky practiced responding.

She was fine until Linda started to talk. At that moment Becky began to holler, kick, and stretch about. Something was obviously amiss. A young woman who was assisting her for the day came to the podium and wheeled Becky screaming into the hallway. They were back almost as quickly as they had left, Becky with a broad smile, out of her chair and walking (with the assistance of the aide holding her arms). Apparently, she had made a commotion because *she didn't want to be in her wheelchair.* She wanted to sit in a regular chair like the other panelists and had gotten upset that she had not been so placed before her mother began to speak. This one example of Becky's communicating her wants also illustrated the need for a sensitive interpretation of her sounds and motions, not an assumption that her outburst was just a tantrum unrelated to what was going on around and inside her.

As for Catherine, few people seemed to want to *interpret* her. Her life seemed a combination of boredom, random activities, and behavior modification. The Woronkos wondered whether she had any future. Her day-to-day circumstances seemed far removed from the interesting school and classroom scenes that her father had seen the principal from Hamilton display. Stan visited Catherine's school one day as an observer and took a camera to record a typical day. He saw a grouping of students that mixed eight-year-olds with twenty-year-olds. At one point a staff member read the group a nursery rhyme. For a music class of seventeen students in the gymnasium, the principal played the piano, and each student had a percussion instrument. "They were encouraged to just bang away and make any noise they wanted," Stan recalls. "It was complete chaos." The principal played a "childish type song." Catherine was sitting on the floor, apparently bored. A staff person was beside her to keep her from getting up. At other times he observed Catherine staring at the ceiling for as much as an hour at a time. Then she would whine when staff would try to make her set the table or pour some lemonade. "She would be sort of crying [as if to complain] but not convincingly."

Life at home was a little better, but not much. For years the Woronkos have been involved in various training programs, learning the do's and don'ts of behavior modification. It was a difficult regimen for the parents:

> We were so tired at coming home after work and going
> through all the behavior modification stuff, the observations,
> the rewards. If she was playing with an object and she wasn't
> putting it in her mouth, we might come over and say, "Good
> girl, Catherine." We might hug her and make the situation
> pleasant. The approach would involve being indifferent if she
> was doing chewing. Or I might say, "No, Catherine," and pull
> it away from her mouth. If she did it three times, we might
> take it away.

The stress of carrying out the program became so great that when an opportunity arose for Catherine to live in a group home in their own neighborhood on weekdays, the Woronkos seized it. But their sense of frustration did not disappear. The behavioral approach of the group home—which they were expected to replicate on weekends—seemed too controlling:

> They [the staff] were looking at it too narrowly. They wanted
> to use very methodical approaches, monitoring, observations
> . . . a scientific measurement approach . . . to get her out of
> her chewing. There would be either random or set intervals in
> an hour or a day when we would be counting the frequency of
> the undesirable or desired behavior. Sometimes the staff would

literally have stopwatches hanging from their waists, and if they were supposed to count how many times something happened in five minutes, they would actually use it. They were very proud. They had graphs and charts too.

To be sure, Catherine's whining and complaining were annoying, even "quite distressful," but Stan was not convinced that behavioral management helped. He compared Catherine's situation to that of a worker whose boss supervises, constrains, and controls the worker's every move; such a management style could quickly evoke a revolt. Perhaps Catherine found behavior management annoying, even intolerable. As we will see, her behavior ultimately changed rather markedly, leading Stan to wonder how Catherine had endured so much close, mechanistic treatment: "Looking back, in some ways she was very tolerant of all the people, ourselves included, around her who were doing all those things to her, remarkably compliant you know; it's surprising because she could have revolted much more. I admire her for that."

Achieving Change

Stan Woronko and Linda Till belong to parent organizations and advocacy groups that promote the right of children with severe disabilities to attend regular school classes. Neither believes that children are really given "clinical judgment" when schools make placement decisions. Rather, schools impose a template of special, regular, and resource programs on students, depending on their labels. Special programs are offered on a take-it-or-leave-it basis. Consequently, both parents resorted to developing strategies to get what they want for their children.

Parents who advocate regular class placement for their children are in much the same position as special education teachers who want to transfer a student from a special to a regular class: they often feel that they must strike a deal with a sympathetic administrator or teacher; sometimes they must trade something for what they want. The Tills and the Woronkos filed legal appeals on behalf of their daughters. Agreement to drop the litigation became some-

thing that the parents could exchange for a reasonably good placement. Stan Woronko describes the maneuvering for a deal. He and
his wife, Marthe, decided that if the public school board would not
integrate Catherine in regular classes in a regular high school, they
would send her to the Catholic school. In Canada, Catholics can
choose to have their taxes support the public *or* the Catholic
schools. The one complication was that the Woronkos' son, who
was already attending the public high school, would be forced to
move to the Catholic school as well if the Woronkos switched their
taxes—families may not split their taxes between parochial and
public schools. It was a bind. "This is where the tactics come in,"
Stan explains.

> Their response to the first phase of our human rights com-
> plaint was literally as thick as a phone book. They were saying
> that this was a frivolous case. We did not consider it frivolous.
> I brought along a lawyer with me from the Advocacy Re-
> source Center for the Handicapped who had been involved in
> the case, but just as an observer. Then, I offered that I would
> drop this case if the school board would keep my son if we
> switched our taxes, for as long as he wished, without payment.
> They went for it. They signed the papers.

The problems with striking such deals are numerous. The pursuit of a deal may force parents to pay an emotional price: many
resent having to bargain individually when they know that the entire system of deciding the appropriate education for a student with
disabilities needs reforming. Also, the deal that is possible may not
be all that the parents want. The situation of Becky Till captures
these difficulties. Whatever deal the Tills manage to strike, Becky
may not really "win." Rather than accept a segregated class, the
Tills have kept Becky out of school altogether. They argued that
she would be harmed by the proposed placement, and she would
be harmed by staying out of school; therefore, the school must act
to remedy the situation. And even though they were in violation of
compulsory education laws, the Tills would not allow the school
board to approve their teaching Becky at home as an alternative: "It
would be an easy out for them to do nothing"—that is, if the Tills

educated her at home, the school would be off the hook with respect to developing a program. As long as she is out of school and not attending an approved program, the school board "still has an obligation to send her to school," Linda Till explains.

Faced with a standoff, the school board has proposed a compromise—not what the Tills wanted but difficult to reject. The board offered Becky a place in the program she had previously attended, the one in which the other students were labeled multihandicapped but in fact were able to walk and talk independently. One bothersome aspect of the offer is that it might occur at another child's expense: "I think they are going to move one kid out because they have maximum capacity [class sizes are set by legal regulations]; they are just going to shuffle one kid out," Linda conjectures—and probably not for purposes of mainstreaming but rather to segregate him further.

Yet the Tills worry that even if they proceed with the appeal and win, any court order in their favor could be stayed while the board pursued an appeal. Achieving a final decision could take years. In addition, like the U.S. Supreme Court in the Rowley case, Canadian courts set serious constraints on the kinds of arguments that complainants can make. The Tills know they are not guaranteed success; indeed, the school board's offer to return Becky to her original special class placement may be unchallengeable, even though the Tills regard it as unacceptable:

> It would be very difficult for us to prove that it would be harmful unless we had documented proof that being in that class before was harmful to her. And in that sense, the only thing we can argue is that she didn't develop as much as we think she could have if she was in an integrated environment. But there is no proof. Just claims. In court you have to support your claims. So we are struggling with the whole issue.

Their struggle is not over what they believe but about how to achieve what they want. By deferring to clinical judgment, society says in effect, "The school can do what it wants so long as the student can reasonably be expected to benefit from the instruction." The Tills are rediscovering what they have known all along, that the phrase "clinical judgment" refers to the school board's perspective, whereas such terms as "opinion" and "claims" refer to the parents' perspective.

To make a case in court, they must transform opinion into fact. Thus, to demonstrate that Becky could benefit from attending a regular class, the Tills point to a child named John who has needs similar to Becky's and who has integrated successfully in the same district. Like Becky, he needs assistance getting in and out of his chair. He needs to be fed and needs help in going to the bathroom. He needs assistance in handling a pencil and paper. He needs assistance with language and communication (although unlike Becky he can talk and thereby demonstrate his intelligence). An aide is assigned to the class to assist him in his program. The Tills charge that the board acts arbitrarily by refusing to provide similar aide service and similar integration to Becky. In addition, the Tills cite the fact that the Catholic school board in the same region successfully integrates students who are as severely disabled as Becky in regular classes.

Catherine Woronko is one example. When she enrolled in regular classes at the local Catholic school, her life changed. A teaching assistant helped gather a group of students in the school to support her integration. They went to classes with her, including physical education, home economics, drama, and typing. Catherine began to fidget less. She appeared less nervous. She stopped much of her whining. She stopped nearly all of her chewing. She began to smile more. Her transformation was not always easily secured, but the fact that Catherine could attend a regular high school and make significant strides in her learning casts doubt on the validity of segregationist judgments. This is what we have come to call the "twin argument": if two students have similar needs and one has been successfully integrated in school, then is it not possible for the other to benefit from integration as well?

Belief, Not Judgment

The idea that professionals can exercise expert judgment suggests that a "best" or "right" judgment can be objectively or scientifically identified. Yet in matters of daily living—for example, where students attend school, how they learn, who they learn with, where a person with a disability can live, whether a person with a disability can secure medical care—the parents interviewed do not regard all professional judgments as "best" or "right" but only as judgments. They recognize the difficulty, even futility, of trying to "prove" the correctness of their own judgments and generally make no pretense of packaging their beliefs as professional judgment. They are satisfied with beliefs: (1) unconditional acceptance should be every child's right; (2) people support one another through community; (3) participation is an essential part of acceptance; and (4) people should not have to pass a test or prove themselves in order to be included in everyday life.

Unconditional Acceptance

Linda Till wants no one to have the authority to place a child with a disability in a nursing home. She believes children belong in their own homes or in foster homes. In a matter such as this, she would defer neither to professional judgment nor to parental prerogative. She would rather stand for what she *believes*, perhaps because she has walked through the wards of nursing homes and has seen children crowded into rooms, children suffering from malnutrition because no one has or takes the time to feed them at a reasonable pace, children suffering from a host of unattended medical needs, children lost from public view: "I can't understand why we have such an aversion to saying to parents, 'Placing your kid in an institution is a rotten thing to do.' It doesn't have to be a right not to be challenged if you are making a choice of something that is clearly harmful. We waffle. We carry on—'Oh you needed support,' and so on. I think we have got to start saying publicly, 'It is wrong.'" Linda Till would not leave decisions of who can live in the community to any individual's judgment. In her mind it ought to be everyone's freedom, protected by society and bequeathed to no one group's discretion, whether parents or professionals. From this perspective, unconditional acceptance—like rejection, segregation, or control—is a value that society can adopt or shun, as it wishes. Linda Till adopts unconditional acceptance as the decent and right thing, even if it cannot be proved "correct" in a scientific sense.

Stan Woronko refers to the high school students in Catherine's new school as having a "natural way" with her and as being willing to say, "That's the way she is." They have tried to stop her from putting things in her mouth, but more important, they have involved her in their world. She has been invited to parties; she sits with other students on the lawn at recess. They accompany her to classes; often another student uses a spare period or study hall to go with Catherine to typing class or home economics. Stan remarks on the changes that have resulted:

> As time went on, Catherine became much more relaxed. Some of the behaviors we had been observing, like the chewing, just went down for no apparent reason. Her basic state and mood is relaxed. She is not tense. She still puts things in her mouth, but the things that are lying around the house, she does not necessarily chew them. We still have problems with the occasional magazine. For some reason, she likes to play with containers for cassettes. She will move them to her mouth and touch them with her tongue or mouth. So that's an annoying habit, and we keep telling her not to do it. You used to have to shout and be almost threatening. If we say "out" she will move it away from her lips. I cannot prove that it's due to the more relaxed, more natural atmosphere that she finds herself in that she's more motivated to explore around her, but I believe it is.

At home, Catherine now has figured out how to turn on the stereo set. She enjoys music. She has discovered the volume control and likes to turn it to loud; she has blown the speaker fuses on several occasions. This new skill can be annoying, but it is also a sign that Catherine is exploring her world. Stan and Marthe have observed Catherine fiddling with the television as well. Their set has pushbuttons, which she has begun to press, experimenting. Stan concludes, "When she has her mind set on some target that she wants to achieve, she's willing to explore and learn. That's in some circumstances. In other circumstances, that might be hard to see and you would assume it is not there." Catherine also seems to have become more initiating. For example, one evening she came to Stan, who was sitting at the computer at home, and pulled on his arm. When he did not respond, she reached over to his other arm as well and pulled him to the closet to get their coats to go outside. This was in marked contrast to her previous moaning or whining.

Community of Support

The students in Catherine's circle of friends or supporters were shown how to interact with her by Annemarie Ruttiman and Marsha Forest, two educators active in the school integration social movement. As a result of this exposure and their own experiences, the students learned how to communicate their acceptance of Catherine. Stan Woronko refers to it as a "natural way." Whether it was natural or learned, they seemed attentive to Catherine's needs. For example, a group of the students reported to Mr. Woronko that one of the aides was unnecessarily rough with Catherine:

> Instead of using it as a teaching opportunity and saying, "Catherine, lets go to your gym class or to your locker" . . . the aide would simply grab her by the hand and pull her and take her there. Without even realizing it, the aide would stop teaching her. At times the aide was rather rough with her simply because she would not walk as fast as the aide wanted. This to me was an indicator that the aide was not in the spirit of what we were trying to accomplish.

Five teaching assistants quit that year. Stan Woronko believes that none would have quit if they had come to understand Catherine and to accept her.

He regards the high school experience as a reawakening for Catherine and also for himself and Marthe. Catherine now has two relatively accepting communities around her: her friends at school, and her family. Stan Woronko wonders, as we might, whether similar communities of support will emerge or can be found for Catherine once she leaves school. He is uncertain about her future, though he knows that he would like a continuing atmosphere of acceptance for Catherine:

> We think about the future. And I do realize that it's the school community that's the glue that holds this together. Once they leave high school, maybe these people will no longer stay in touch. So those who are in the circle right now may not necessarily meet anymore. We are hoping that some of them might be interested in maintaining some sort of relationship, but its not something that one can in any way plan.

In other words, acceptance means more than allowing a person to move into the community; it may also mean people forming communities around one another.

Participation

Similarly, acceptance should mean more than passive recognition of a person's presence within a group or in a given place. The person must be encouraged to participate. And it cannot be, Linda Till says, a one-time or sometime event; it must be constant

> in every single thing that goes on in her [Becky's] life. It's constant. It's ongoing. By "every single event" I mean every single event. I don't just mean a dinner party that we have on a Saturday night, the television we turn on once in a while, or going to the restaurant, but . . . if I'm picking her up out of her chair to carry her somewhere, Becky has to participate by positioning herself, and by trying to walk; if she wants to get from her bed to the floor, she has to participate.

The Tills have struggled to get Becky to take an active part in the small and large aspects of her life. Initially, she resisted; Linda says, "We fought for a long time." But eventually, Becky agreed to participate. Now she stands up to get out of her chair. She helps do the dishes. In fact, she gets angry if she is not involved in the full range of household activities. When Linda Till speaks in public about her family and Becky's progress, she highlights the concept of participation with a bit of drama. She tells her audience, "It would be as ludicrous to expect Becky to learn from the regular curriculum as to expect her to water ski." Then she flashes a slide on the screen which shows Becky and her mother together, being pulled on a windsurfer behind a powerboat. The point? "With adaptation and support she can do anything." In other words, participation is not something someone needs to prove themselves worthy or capable of; it is something that one should have, unconditionally, as part of being accepted and valued. Further, if adaptations and support are necessary to accomplish even partial participation, then they should be made available.

Acceptance Without Proof of Worth

Proving oneself is a common theme in the lives of people with disabilities. It is the opposite of unconditional acceptance. For example, students must prove their eligibility for participation in typical classes. In a now classic story of one person's struggle to leave an institution and to win the right to assistance in communication, Anne McDonald, a young woman who has athetoid cerebral palsy, had to prove her intelligence before government inquiries and commissions in Melbourne, Australia (Crossley and McDonald 1980). Rosemary Crossley, an employee at the institution where Anne was living, decided to try to teach a group of nonverbal, presumably severely intellectually disabled children. She developed simple communication systems. As several of the students, Anne in particular, began to respond, she was able to make the systems more complex and eventually to employ a language board showing the alphabet and selected, frequently used words. Anne and other children revealed unexpected literacy. The only difficulty was that other people in the institution, from many fellow teachers up to the superintendent, believed that Rosemary was manipulating the students, because her technique involved supporting the child's arm during communication. The others would not accept the possibility that Anne was not severely intellectually disabled. Eventually, Rosemary and Anne won their struggle, but not until Anne was forced, time and again, to prove her ability.

Stan Woronko now believes that the years he and Marthe and

many dedicated (and some not so dedicated) teachers spent trying
to manage Catherine's behaviors, trying to get her to do small tasks
before permitting her to be part of typical events of children her
age, were a mistake. Many times she complied with the training
efforts, but just as often she resisted. He sees acceptance without
passing a test for access as a prerequisite to Catherine's being motivated to learn, explore, and participate: "Create an environment
where there is a lot of opportunity, and responsiveness and sensitivity, and sort of have her lead the way as to what she likes and
wants to learn. That's what they have been doing in the school." In
other words, being part of community life—for example, high
school classes and socializing—comes first. Skills can be developed
in that context, around the activities in which the person shows an
interest.

Still another way to look at this issue is that Becky and Catherine, like Anne McDonald, refuse to participate or to demonstrate
their ability to do so until people around them have proved *them-*
selves. Catherine have been communicating this through her tantrums, whining, resistance to being pulled, and so forth. Becky
shows it by keeping her feelings and abilities to herself until she is
sure that she can trust the people around her. Linda Till refers to it
as Becky's sense of feeling safe. This was a sensible strategy for self-
preservation at the nursing home, where, for a person who is not
verbal, efforts to participate might appear as wild sounds and ges-
ticulations, too easily interpreted as acting out. It was "safer" *not* to
demonstrate skills: "If you made a sound, you were stomped on,"
Linda remembers. "If you could move, you were strapped down. If
you walked, you were punished—they said you might step on the
other kids, and some did. Making sounds, moving, walking, that's a
disruptive kid" in the nursing home. "They saw them as bodies that
they had to control; [so] you tied kids down, you hit kids, you
punished them," she asserts. When Becky feels safe, she does perform or, more accurately, she does participate. But if she must perform before being allowed to participate, she generally refuses. At
home she feels safe. At school, in doctors' offices, and in many
other places, she does not.

Linda Till remembers when her boss first told her about the

book *Annie's Coming Out* (Crossley and McDonald 1980): "She said, it's Becky," Linda recalls. And it was, even down to the drawings in the book showing Annie twisted, head back, precisely as Linda Till had found Becky in the nursing home. The book recounts numerous occasions when Anne McDonald refused to prove to people who were testing her, or those who assumed that she lacked intelligence, that she knew the communication system Rosemary Crossley had introduced her to. Becky knows how to resist in precisely the same ways:

> It was three years from the time that Becky learned to walk until she *would* walk in front of her doctor. Even then I had to bribe her [by promising to take her out to dinner after the exam]. Well, that was worth giving in for. She flew. She ran. She walked for a nurse who knew nothing about how to support her for walking. She did it anyway. Once she decided to do it, she did a phenomenal job. She had been denied surgery for three years because the doctors did not define her as a walker [and they would not take the parents' word for it], and therefore such an aggressive procedure was not justified. [But when the doctor saw her walking] he said on the spot, "Well I guess we better do the surgery."

Becky's mobility improved dramatically after the operation. Nevertheless, Linda Till believes that it was wrong to approach Becky as someone who had to pass a test to receive treatment. She knows that Becky's "defenses are great," but she accuses the doctors of bias in deciding to do surgery only on those people who can demonstrate some ability to walk. Also, she blames them for not helping Becky feel safe. "It's the same with communication," Linda explains. "She's got it down pat. You know, cross your eyes, stick your tongue out, and look at the ceiling."

Ironically, once Becky feels accepted unconditionally, without having had to prove herself, she relishes performing. She participates in Girl Guides (the Canadian equivalent of Girl Scouts). Recently her "patrol" mates elected her seconder, or vice-chairperson. Here she earns badges by accomplishing various tasks. The Guides accommodate people with disabilities: any child can pursue and achieve any badge. The process of accommodation does not have a name, but Linda Till refers to it as the principle of "equally challenging": "Each child, regardless of disabilities, is entitled to pass any test and earn any badge no matter how modified you have to make the tasks." Since one consistent means of communication available to Becky at this time is to give "yes" and "no" responses, the testers must learn how to ask yes-and-no questions, or to set up choices from which she can select. In the test on flowers, for example, instead of going through pictures of wild flowers and asking Becky to name them, the tester asked her to focus her gaze on the comment she wanted to make about a particular flower, from a prepared list of choices. Recently, she finished the flower badge requirements, being tested by an examiner who was previously unknown to her. Linda describes the situation as supportive but difficult:

> Initially, she wasn't that comfortable . . . with a person she had never met. But they said, "Now take your time, give it a try," and she did proceed to answer her questions perfectly properly and to do matches. And that's a major accomplishment for her to answer questions in a pressure situation where people are expecting certain things of her. She really was so excited. It was like she crossed a hurdle . . . a communication hurdle.

Of course, this was a different kind of hurdle from the school assessments that had been imposed on her before. In the flowers test, she had to show that she knew certain material in order to qualify for the badge. In the school access tests, she was asked to perform in order to prove her worth as a person. In one instance she was already accepted; in the other many professionals and much of society were sitting in judgment to decide whether she was worthy of acceptance.

The Professional Role Reexamined

In his remarkably troubling book *The Case Worker* (1976), George Konrad presents a picture that is at once real and surreal. Through the perspective of the protagonist, a "caseworker-gone-native" (that is, one who identifies with his clients, to the point—in this instance—of becoming a surrogate father for one), we enter the lives of society's refuse and those who discard or manage the refuse. Other people's troubles fill the caseworker's head, enter his dreams, and make his own equanimity a mirage. His best clients, his "heroes," are those who solve their own problems, those who don't call back, those for whom troubles are an aberration in otherwise normal lives. But new cases populate his files faster than he can close out the old ones.

The caseworker's ever accumulating cases, all calls of desperation, are like the ever mounting instances of conflict the Tills and Woronkos encounter with bureaucracies. Their lives would be so much simpler if every school and every teacher wanted their children. They would love not having to call back agency after agency, school after school, and doctor after doctor to secure basic services. They want society to accommodate people with disabilities as well as it accommodates the rest of the population. Becky would not have nearly starved to death or have had an undiagnosed problem in her esophagus if she had not been dumped in a nursing home where the administrator attributed her exceptionally low weight to her cerebral palsy. Life would have been easier for Becky if she had been seen as someone to understand and as someone who wanted to contribute. Catherine could have avoided years of the rigid training to eliminate what were largely her own behavioral signs of frustration and boredom if the schools had known how much she wanted to be around other students, to have friends, and to be part of everyday life. The Tills and Woronkos have no inner need to be exceptional advocates or change agents, but they feel they have no choice.

Konrad's book describes the caseworker entering a one-room apartment where the father of a child with severe retardation has just committed suicide. Should he abandon his own family and middle-class life, including the caseworker-and-manager role, to become this feral child's keeper? And if he doesn't care for Feri—with all his feces-smearing, screaming, and babbling—who will? Society's usual, single choice seems to be to deposit such a child in an institution. The rules of the caseworker's job, even the ethics of his profession, require nothing more than detached orderliness on his part: "I am bound only to take the unattended minor to the place specified in the directive." Yet he knows the consequences: "If they accepted him, Feri would disappear through the trap door leading to the repository for infantile rubbish, just as adult rubbish is consigned by the social order to . . . mental hospitals and prisons or to old people's homes . . . [to wait] for . . . death" (Konrad 1976, 70).

Becky and Catherine are not like Feri, although it is not at all clear what he might become if given other opportunities. Konrad implies that Feri cannot change, that his existence is burdensome; perhaps Konrad characterizes Feri as somewhat unidimensional because his intent is to reveal not the child but rather the caseworker. We really never come to know Feri as a person; he appears from a distance as someone in great need, but we never glimpse what his world looks like to him. Rather, "we are a system of human services that treats people as surplus and that relegates the beleaguered caseworker's job to compiling records of failure and selling indifference and normalcy" (Konrad 1976, 65). The indifference he sells is society's insulation against seeing or feeling misery, its denial that some people suffer insufferably. Normalcy involves helping people tolerate the intolerable. Yet Konrad's caseworker finds that he cannot be the good soldier whose job it is to create a kind of demilitarized zone between the affected and unaffected. Pondering the troubling questions that plague all caseworkers and all human service agents for whom socialization to the professional role has not completely obliterated personal identification with victims' lives, he knows he must abandon the role of peacekeeper and manager. He must forsake his own orderly life and instead commit himself to the genuineness of doing something meaningful for Feri. In this, he is like the Tills and Woronkos.

Konrad has no grand solution. He warns against the quick fix or "fast start": in other words, marginal or illusory reforms. He resigns himself to being the humble bureaucrat, the consummate listener: "My highest aspiration is that a medium-rank, utterly insignificant civil servant should, as far as possible, live with his eyes open" (Konrad 1976, 177), see suffering and commiserate with it, create dialogue where others are mute, and at least admit our common humanity.

CHAPTER VI

A Case of Inclusion:
Individual or Schoolwide Change?

MELVIN'S INTRODUCTION (Chapter II) was set in the context of questioning whether parents are romantics or realists. Mary Lou, Melvin's adoptive mother, like other parents in this book, is a visionary, seeing a world for Mel that only slightly resembles the world so regularly imposed on him by others. As he grows up, she and Melvin together create and try to make real their vision of an inclusive world.

When Melvin finished the fifth grade, Mary Lou decided to move to Massachusetts to be nearer to her aging parents. But for families with handicapped children, moving is not simple. Before she could decide on a new location, she had to find a school where the staff would approach Mel with an open mind.

The experiences that Mary Lou relates do not reveal an ideal school situation but do include numerous instances in which she and Melvin achieved an approximation of her vision of integration. Their experiences in the new community and their efforts to create school integration provide us with a vivid picture of what one school *is* like for a student classified as disabled. (Chapter VII describes what education *could* be like if schools fully adopted a philosophy of inclusion.)

One of Melvin's sisters lives in a Catholic institution. He has two other sisters, one who has been adopted and one up for adoption. Clinical reports say that like Mel, Annie, his institutionalized sister, was abused by their father. Child-care authorities consider her too disturbed to be adoptable. Perhaps if Mel were still institutionalized, they would consider him "unadoptable" as well. Mel talks about this sister; he remembers that she would give him his cereal for breakfast. Mary Lou has pictures of Mel's mother and father which she intends to share with him when he is older. He has not had any contact with them since he was institutionalized. She thinks that some day he will probably want to see his mother, but so far he has not asked to. One of the things that Mel likes about his new home is, in his words, that "Daddy not know where Massachusetts is." On other occasions, Mel insists that he does not have a father. Mary Lou thinks that he harbors a deep of fear of his father. He becomes very upset when he sees men drinking any kind of alcoholic beverage.

Obviously, Mel carries his father with him. One day while he and his teacher were at a fast food hamburger shop, Mel suddenly got down on the floor and began laughing hysterically—not a happy laugh but a nervous one. When the teacher became upset and tried to get him to stand up, Mel became even more anxious. He started screaming and tipped over food trays. The teacher had to remove him physically from the restaurant, still not knowing what had upset Mel so. Later, Mary Lou figured it out: a woman at a nearby table had slapped her three-year-old, and apparently Mel reacted in fear. Perhaps the incident reminded him of his father.

Kids' Worlds: Being Normal, Being Friends

By chance, the block to which Mary Lou moved has five children Mel's age. They are all in his homeroom, and one girl, Kim, has become a best friend. Mel calls her that: "My best friend." The night before the first school dance, Kim came to his house with some records to teach him how to dance; she also instructed him on which records were considered especially "cool." Mary Lou volunteered to chaperon the dance, "to sort of keep an eye on things." It was a typical middle school dance. The boys sat on one side of the gym. The girls sat on the other side. Once the dancing began, Mel crossed the floor several times to ask girls to dance, and several girls asked him to dance.

The new school has been even better for Mel than his previous school in terms of what Mary Lou calls "the social thing." She attributes this in part to the good fortune of landing in a neighborhood of sixth graders *and* to the simpler ways of rural living. "You know I think back to the summer, and all the kids got really into building a tree house," she relates. Mel and his friends collected scrap wood from the different parents in the area, and for three weekends they worked on the project. This and other "less sophisticated" play (that is, not organized by adults and not as competitive as the games and activities of the children in the city where they had lived formerly) allows Mel to participate more easily than before. He always has attracted friends, but he often had difficulty taking part in more structured activities; city life may have had more options for children, but if Mel did not fit into them, their availability did not matter.

At first, Mel was nervous at his new school. This showed in various ways, but especially in his communication. He would say very little when he first arrived. He spoke in "one word sentences," Mary Lou explains. Then he slowly relaxed. The more comfortable and familiar he became with school and other students, the more he spoke. Mary Lou smiles as she relates that school staff think Mel has made "amazing progress" in language since coming to the school. She attributes his "progress" to his feeling accepted.

Typically, fellow students understand Mel's speech better than adults do. For one thing, they spend more time with him, and therefore become more accustomed to his speech. People who know him well can understand almost everything he says; strangers can't understand him at all. Also, since his friends and classmates experience events with him, they often grasp the context of his speech. Mary Lou explains, "He's really funny. He'll come home and try to tell me a story, and if I can't figure out what he's talking about, he'll say call Adam or call Kim. I have to call one of the other kids to figure out what he is telling me."

Mel's enthusiasm for communication seems related to his sense of "making the grade" socially. Having asked to have homework like the other students, he decided one evening not to do it—and was thrilled because he was punished for not doing the work: "He had to sit on the wall and miss recess like all the other kids [who failed to do their homework]." "Me sit on wall," Mel announced to Mary Lou. "No do homework." Fortunately, he did not like the wall-sitting experience enough to want to avoid homework every night. He has not missed again.

Mel's attitude toward school is much like that of other students. He bounds off to school with great enthusiasm. Yet if you ask him whether he likes school, he says no, without any sense of contradiction. Mel says he likes homeroom best—the half-hour each day when he has an opportunity to socialize with friends. He also likes his "downtown days" when he goes into the community to learn how to cross streets safely, how to ride the bus, how to order at a restaurant, and so forth. Clearly, "doing things" is easier and more motivating for Mel than reading and other academic subjects—although, as we will see, he has been successful in academic work as well, particularly where he participates with a group.

Professionals' Worlds

Mel still has his moments. He has been really into roller skating. We have this big rink in town. And he's into strobe lights and rock music. He'll be out there skating away. Its really great in terms of his energy level. Then all of a sudden he'll disappear. I'll discover he just got into the disk jockey booth. And I'll have to go and make sure he gets out of there. He has less dangerous "impulsivity" now, but it's still inappropriate at times.

Such events make Mel seem different from other students, and some might see that difference as justification for treating him differently, especially in determining when and how he learns. Mary Lou responds first by interpreting his actions. "When he's real frustrated he might resort to banging his head, but not with the intensity he used to. I usually can tell why, or eventually he will give us a cue."

Mary Lou chose to live in "a really small community of about nine hundred people" because the school seemed flexible. Although

it had few programs for children with disabilities, people there
seemed willing to adapt to Melvin. She felt that his chances of being treated as more "typical" than "special" were greater in this
district than in larger, more sophisticated ones (that is, those with
more specialized programs). She thought that the school (comprising kindergarten through eighth grade) was good for "typical" students and therefore would probably be good for Mel. Nevertheless,
not having had a student "even remotely like Melvin" before, the
school staff and administrators were understandably anxious. The
principal expressed the concern: "We'll give it a try but I don't
know how we are going to pull this off and make it work." As
noted earlier, teachers in newly integrated schools often state that
they are insufficiently trained for integration and complain about
parents' or administrators' expectations. But such teachers generally
do not want to participate, and many have turned down training
opportunities. Aware of this and similar research findings, Mary
Lou wondered whether the principal's cautious statement really
meant that she was assuming integration would not work for Mel
and that she was edging toward an ultimate decision to send him to
the special program in a nearby district. Also voicing concern that
the other students might be "victimized," the principal was in effect
saying that the *regular* students belong; Melvin is *different* and can
stay in the school so long as he does not disrupt their education. In
short, if the integration process did not go smoothly, Mel—not the
school—would be responsible. The principal's warning, then, communicated that Melvin's presence in the school was an experiment
that could be canceled.

During the first few weeks of school, Mary Lou would get
phone calls—"He's out of control. You'd better come"— and she
would have to leave her own teaching in a neighboring district to
handle each crisis. "I would leave my class and run up there. And it
would be horrendous. He would be throwing books at people and
lying on the ground, and I'd walk in the room and he'd jump up
and sit at his desk and say, 'Hi Mary Lou,' as if to say, 'I'm all right;
I'm being perfectly fine here.' People would look at me and say,
'Wow.' He was running them around." Mary Lou interpreted these
episodes as stemming from Melvin's anxiety with the new school

and as testing the teachers to discover the limits for student behavior. She talked with them about it, and together they agreed to take a harder line with Mel, communicating to him that he would have to adhere to school rules. Within a week of having limits set, he was fine.

Just as the principal worried about whether the school could make itself work for Melvin, other parents expressed deep concern; at a parent-teacher meeting one parent asked Mary Lou whether Melvin could be dangerous. Angered, she wanted to respond, "No, but I can be." But several months later, parents and the principal, as well as many of the teaching staff, seemed to have grown comfortable with Melvin. This new-found acceptance posed another kind of problem:

> The principal has become a real advocate, so now I have to guard against them babying him. That's a major frustration too. I think being one of the only handicapped kids [means] everyone can get too paternalistic. If the principal is talking to the superintendent in the hall, Mel interrupts her to stop and talk in a way that other kids would not be allowed. Or I see teachers say, "Let me do that for you," things that he could perfectly well do. I was walking through the lunch room [one day], and one of the teachers was getting his tray for him, helping him put his food on the tray. I saw it and said, "Go get your own lunch." He's been able to do that for years. He's been doing it ever since, now. But it was just one of those things where he just played into their assumptions, and nobody knew he was capable of it.

Mary Lou did not assume that Melvin could do the same work that every other student could do, but at the same time she did not want him unnecessarily limited. At times her worry turned to frustration and even resentment. Some people talked to her as if she were denying Mel's "real" disabilities and difficulties. "You need to be realistic," people told her. "He's a *very* handicapped little kid." In its efforts to put a label on Mel, the school seemed to be forcing Mary Lou into a false choice. If she "admitted" to Mel's being severely handicapped, as some people believed, it could mean that he would become a kind of school mascot, infantilized for being different. His uniqueness would become a sign of cuteness and dependence. If, on the other hand, she refused to acquiesce to the label "very handicapped," people were ready to label *her* confused, unrealistic, and therefore not well suited to decide about what was best for Mel educationally. Mary Lou understood the confusion around her—she did not discount Mel's various difficulties—but she wanted him to have an ordinary, if supported, school life.

From the start, despite the district's seeming flexibility and its actual efforts to create a program for Melvin at the local school, many people in the district believed he would be better off in a neighboring district that had a program especially for students with disabilities.

> All last year they kept wanting to send Mel to North Adams, thinking they just had much more to offer him. I went down and looked at that program and was absolutely horrified. The class that they had in mind for Melvin had an excellent teacher. She had experience in autism, with Clara Park [author of the book *The Siege*]. But this teacher had four kids who were all nonverbal . . . and limited in other ways. The age range was from nine to seventeen. They were in a portable classroom behind the rest of the school. The only mainstreaming was at lunch, but here too they were really separated from other students. The four kids went to the cafeteria and ate at their own table.

In such a place, Mel's segregation would be nearly complete. He would not hear or converse with other students, and he would be twenty miles from his home district and his neighborhood friends. "This was a case of the teacher being very skilled but the situation being wrong," Mary Lou explains. Apart from being sent to a special school or institution, it was as out of the mainstream as a student might ever get. A hallway scene during her visit to the North Adams school confirmed her belief: "I heard one of the kids [who has no disability] say, 'Oh here comes the retard class.' The principal was walking with us at the time, and he didn't respond. He just didn't deal with it. I thought, 'Nope, Mel's not coming here.'"

Still, the school district's idea of transferring Mel somewhere else or placing him under specialists' care in his local school seemed to Mary Lou designed in a genuine effort to help him, not to discriminate against him. Concerned about his needs, the school placed Mel in a resource room half-time along with the only other child in the school who has a noticeable disability—Down syndrome. The rest of the time he attended a regular class. After about a month, the school hired an aide to help Mel participate with the other fifth graders, and he began to spend more time in the regular class. Mary Lou thought the program was good for Mel. But the school was prohibited from implementing any community instruction for him; state regulations did not allow noncertified staff such as the teaching assistant to take students off school grounds. Also, the school continued to worry that Mel was not getting enough instruction directed at his "special" needs. Eventually, the principal hired a special education teacher. This allowed Mel to have the community instruction and to be supported in the regular class, yet it also reinforced Mel's separate status in the school: "What happens is that the regular educators get less and less involved in Mel's program," Mary Lou concludes. "It's like [the special education teacher] is the expert. And unfortunately, his background or commitment is not toward mainstreaming." The special teacher became Mel's primary teacher.

Mary Lou kept interjecting integrationist ideas into the teachers' and principal's discussion of how to teach Mel. She talked with them about encouraging the special education teacher to lend a hand with the "regular" students in order to give the program more flexibility and to make Melvin seem less like an outsider. That idea has had little effect, apparently because the special education teacher prefers to operate on his own. He rejected a sixth grade teacher's suggestion that Melvin join his class to work on a science project, apparently feeling that Mel could not handle it. But when Mary Lou brought a documentary video on mainstreaming to show to the teachers, speech therapist, principal, and others, they were excited:

[The speech therapist] started bringing him into the English class and doing adaptations. On Monday the regular English

teacher was reading an O'Henry story. For the ending, she had
the kids all write their own endings. So the speech therapist
helped Mel dictate his ending. Then she helped him type it on
the word processor. He shared his ending when all the other
kids got up and shared theirs. I think she is really modeling
that [adapting curricula] for everyone else [the other teachers].

The school's approach with Melvin remained cautious, however. He was allowed into the regular "special" classes such as music, art, and gym, and of course lunch and recess, but except for
English he went to special classes for the balance of his time in
school. The district was perhaps different from many in its willingness to integrate Mel in at least some subjects, but its concerns
about adequately serving him in the local school and its willingness
to send him off to a special class for his academic work reveal a
trepidation about taking new directions. Wanting the school to respond differently, Mary Lou made suggestions, showed a film,
brought in experts, and encouraged staff to visit other integration
programs. She wanted the school to approach Mel as an interesting
and capable child, someone whose development it wanted to help.
She wanted the school to share her desire to have Mel participate in
every school routine and event. Integration would not work, she
reasoned, if she constantly had to generate new integration strategies, and if she had to persuade teachers to collaborate.

Mel's status in school had analogues in other areas. For example, Mary Lou could not easily find sitters for Mel: people felt they
needed professional expertise to care for him. Even the respite
agency Mary Lou called was unable to find a qualified person.
Months passed. When Mary Lou asked whether the agency could
hire college students, she was told that Mel's needs were too great,
his "behavior too challenging," for an inexperienced person. For his
part, Mel referred to the woman who ran the respite service as "the
SDC lady," labeling her with the initials of the institution where he
had once lived. When she first came to the house to do an "intake
interview," he blurted out, "Oh no, SDC lady," and presented what
Mary Lou refers to as his "worst show. . . . I had a hard time
convincing her that he didn't have those challenging behaviors all
of the time." Mary Lou felt that professional services too often

viewed Mel as totally different from other people and therefore properly the responsibility and province of specialists only:

> I found it frustrating to get off the phone hearing that "No, there is no one we can find to do this respite," when two twelve-year-old kids next door would come by and say, "Hey, we are going skating at the sand basin. Can Mel come?" And when I say, "Well, I can't come right now," they say, "That's okay, you don't have to come. We can be with Mel. It's fine." So he goes off for two and a half hours' skating with two twelve-year-olds. And it's fine.

Personal Change

In a way, Mel secured his own respite care workers. He has always been infatuated with railroads, and Mary Lou often took him to a state park that has a mini-railroad museum. A staff member there got to know Mel and one day volunteered to spend time with him. Mary Lou also recalls the man back in Syracuse who introduced Mel to model trains. The man operates a twenty-four-hour breakfast restaurant, the Eggplant, which was Melvin's favorite breakfast place. The owner began to invite him behind the counter to cook his own breakfast, and gave him an Eggplant T-shirt. Melvin talked about wanting to become a cook at the restaurant. The owner would tell him he'd have to work his way up: "You have to start off by washing dishes for me for a couple of years first."

The man became Mel's friend; they talked about trains and going to the train station; they looked at pictures of trains that Mel brought to his restaurant. A couple of days before Mary Lou and Mel moved to Massachusetts, the man came to Mary Lou's front door asking for Mel:

> I said . . . he was out with someone. So he said, "Well, just give him this from me and tell him that I knew he would love them more than anybody else I know." He gave Melvin his train set from when he was a little boy. I said, "I know he is going to want to thank you." And the guy said, "No, I don't

think I want to say goodbye to him. Just, could you do me a
favor, write me a card every three or four months and tell me
how he is doing?" . . . We treasure the train set. I only let
Melvin play with it when I'm standing there with him. He can
be rough on that sort of thing.

Mary Lou writes to the man faithfully to report on Melvin's life.

It is hard to know just how much Melvin's friend-getting abilities soften the effects of his occasional tantrums on how people
perceive him and on their willingness to allow him to participate in
their everyday worlds. But it is obviously important to be accepted,
to participate, and to have friends. One day, for example, Mary
Lou and Melvin went to the local state college to go swimming. At
the pool a woman was swimming laps using a snorkel. While Mary
Lou was explaining to him what a snorkel is and how it works, he
started swimming after the snorkel. She saw what was happening
and set out after him, but Melvin is a faster swimmer.

So I'm swimming after him yelling "Melvin. Stop. Stop." He
got to the snorkel before I did. He grabbed it and yelled,
"Hello down there." The woman came up sputtering. She was
really angry. She said, "Young man, what do you think you
are doing?" He got totally echolalic [repeating words he has
heard previously], yelling "you doing" and laughing hysterically. He was really nervous with her anger.

Mary Lou could not simultaneously control or calm Melvin *and*
explain to the furious woman what had happened. Fortunately, "we
have a really good life guard who likes Mel, so while he got Mel to
calm down, I was able to speak to the lady." She too calmed down.

These incidents convey that Melvin's success in participating in
the community is due in part to his skills—he talks to people and
he shows an interest in them and their activities. His acceptance
depends on people's abilities to "understand" him. He becomes understood as people work to get to know him.

Jeff and Cindy Strully have written about this phenomenon of
acceptance in an article about their daughter Shawntell, who has
been labeled severely handicapped. They conclude that despite soci-

ety's emphasis on productivity or competitiveness, her future success in community life may depend not on how many work skills she develops but on friendships and other relationships. They point to Shawntell's closest friend and declare, "It will be the 'Tanya's' of our future who will ensure that all people are an active part of their community." It will be people like Tanya who will see Melvin and Shawntell as legitimate and worthy irrespective of the skills they have and do not have, who become comfortable with them and interested in knowing them, and who make the society "competent to support everyone" (Strully and Strully 1985, 227). The test will be not whether Mel and Shawntell are competent, but whether the culture is competent.

The Strullys suggest that change will occur through individual relationships. Tanya, like Shawntell, has become a different person by virtue of their friendship. She will demand that other people understand and respect her values, even emulate them. When her school principal wrote her a note and "congratulated" her for her friendship with Shawntell, she was offended. She spends time with Shawntell not out of a sense of service or just for Shawntell; she also does it for herself. She enjoys her friend's company. In explaining her motivations to the principal, she became a change agent.

Similarly, Mel's entrance to the new school in Massachusetts marked a time of change. The teachers have been discovering what works for Melvin educationally. They have not given up on writing, which is difficult for him, but they are concentrating more on typing. His reading program focuses mostly on community instruction: for example, identifying the word "Men" on restroom doors, deciphering menus, and role-playing restaurant scenes; two days a week he learns how to get around on the public buses, how to order food, and how to cross streets. During his time in the resource room, students who have no disabilities come to spend time with him—for example, to play games with him on the computer. Mel also works at the school, sorting mail into teachers' mailboxes and making duplicates of instructional materials at the copier. Occasionally, the principal joins Melvin in a sing-a-long by playing the piano. At the end of his first year in the school, the regular fifth grade teacher called Mary Lou to say that she believed it would

have been better for Mel if he had not had his own special education teacher; with only an assistant, he might have been included
more in the class. Apparently, as long as Mel had a special teacher,
the other teachers felt freed from having to plan for Mel or orches-
trate his involvement in the regular curriculum or in relationships
with other students. The fact that the fifth grade teacher called
Mary Lou suggested that Melvin's presence in the school was enabling teachers to think about how such a student could be accommodated and about their own part in the process.

As good as Mel's experience and the school's experience have
been in some respects, we need to consider whether they have been
emblematic of organizational and social change or merely interesting but not very generalizable or enduring developments. Without
Mary Lou's ongoing efforts to effect integration, the school would
probably revert to familiar practice, such as hiring a special education teacher to plan and supervise the whole of Mel's education or
placing him in a special class full time or, worse yet, in a special
class for students with severe disabilities only. As Mary Lou introduced ideas about community instruction, team teaching, and
methods of adapting curricula, the school implemented some of
them, employed compromise versions of others (for example, there
was more willingness to allow parallel teaching than team teaching), and used others as occasional rather than general practices (for
example, adapted curricula were tried experimentally). Mel's presence and Mary Lou's involvement coaxed the school into styles and
locations of instruction that it would probably not have adopted on
its own. Mary Lou introduced consultants; she showed them
models; she described practices she had seen elsewhere. Where the
school has been successful with the new ideas, it takes pride in the
resultant accomplishments and in Mel. At the same time, the school
seems only one student and one parent away from retreating to
familiar, ordinary processes and to the separate, "special" system. In
this respect, Mel's new school is probably not unusual. A general
and enduring transformation has not yet been accomplished; what
such a transformation would entail is the subject of the next
chapter.

CHAPTER VII

The Inclusive School

NOVELIST MARGARET KENNEDY has written about the integrity of the person with a disability when he or she encounters society's "help." Hers is a particularly fine story because it portrays an enduring, completely equal friendship between an artist and a Gertrude Stein–like intellectual. At one point in her novel *Not in the Calendar,* Kennedy's intellectual protagonist describes the principal of a school for deaf children: "Our principal . . . has no use for untrained people. She's a splendid person. Very fierce" (Kennedy 1964, 183). Many students with disabilities would welcome standards of fierce quality. Adrienne Asch discusses this issue at some length in her contribution to the book *Beyond Separate Education* (Lipsky and Gartner 1989). A college student named Zach, who is legally blind, complains about some of his high school teachers. In physics and other classes he was "excused" from lab work, blackboard activities, and the like because his teachers had not prepared a way for him to be included. He wishes his teachers had provided after-school tutoring and advising as a normal part of their responsibilities. "Looking back on it now, I think my teachers couldn't do enough to let me out of things. I didn't care enough to challenge them" (Asch 1989, 185). In short, they were not fierce enough.

Asch cites numerous other examples of lowered expectations. A student in New York City complains that "most kids are below average and pass with exceptionally high marks because they're disabled. Special education . . . passes you with simple work." Chicago special education teachers tell regular class teachers to have students who are blind complete only half the number of math problems assigned to their seeing classmates; Asch finds this an unnecessary accommodation, presumably basing her judgment on her own experience. She criticizes residential schools for not offering as varied and challenging a curriculum as many public schools. A student in the Midwest complains that she was never able to take calculus or chemistry. In contrast, Asch describes other "public school programs that are characterized by perceptive, creative adaptation and a minimum of patronization." She mentions a blind student who was encouraged to do lab work in chemistry and to participate in a two-month exchange as an American Field Service student in Latin America, and a blind high school student who benefits from an itinerant teacher who serves as a consultant to her school's physical education teachers (Asch 1989, 185–89).

Translated to our concern for how schools can best welcome and serve students with disabilities, Asch's and Kennedy's maxim is that people who have disabilities are important people. Students with disabilities deserve school principals who espouse high standards and fierce purpose. They deserve teachers with skill.

The mere physical presence of students with disabilities in schools will not suffice. Grudging acceptance of integration is by definition inadequate. What is needed rather are schools with *fierce* commitment to inclusion, where students with severe disabilities are not only accepted but actually recruited.

This chapter explores what education would look like if it attempted to work from the perspective of the discriminated-against student, the visionary parent, the integrationist teacher. In other words, what would it look like if the Lehrs and Galatis were to create it? What would it look like if an integrationist teacher, parent, or advocate were to transform it?

Politics and Power, Not Treatment and Curricula

Maria and Felicia Galati finally won access and even acceptance in their neighborhood elementary school. The new principal proved supportive, eventually becoming an advocate of inclusion. Yet as

Rose and Dom Galati prepared to send Felicia to high school, they were again forced to become advocates, something that the parents of nondisabled students need not do. Felicia would be the first student with severe disabilities to attend their local high school. The district had integrated students with disabilities into one of its high schools but not Felicia's local school. The school board considered integration a special activity or model confined to a single site. Students "do not go to their neighborhood schools," Rose explains. "They are told to go to the one school that allows some integration. The mix of kids is incredible. They clump the kids in the one school. All of the kids labeled severe were placed there." Ironically, with all of the district schools near full enrollment, students are generally prohibited from attending a school outside their neighborhood boundary, but a different rule applies to students with disabilities. Unless they happen to live near the one integrated school, those whose parents select integration must cross boundaries. Rose believes the board wants Felicia to leave the neighborhood as well, "but I don't think they'll dare even suggest it, because they know we will reject it."

Rose and Dom's strategizing will focus on Felicia's program as well as its location. Rose wants Felicia's schooling to reflect her interests, and she wants Felicia to be with nondisabled students:

> I know what I would like for Felicia. I know the subjects that I would like to see her in. I have no intention and no desire to see her sitting in an algebra class. I truly do not. I want her to take the arts. I want her to be involved in phys. ed. I want her to be involved if possible in some sort of team activity where she can be part of an extracurricular program. She should have religion class. And computers. There should be something there on computers for her. And then I want her to do lots of stuff around the school. Jobs. I want her really to be developing skills around the school.

Rose does not want Felicia in activities that are staged: she does not want her setting a table with cutlery if no one will be eating at it, or making a bed in the classroom where no one sleeps. Instead, she wants her to learn to set her own place in the cafeteria, to eat with friends, to change her clothes when she goes to gym, to walk upstairs independently on her way to classes, and to put on her jacket when she is going outside. At the hairdresser where Felicia sorts curlers and helps with other odd jobs, Rose wants her "to be partners with a high school student on work-study. She can do what she can do, and they can do what they can do."

Rose envisions a time when inclusion is no longer just an "option" but rather an inviolable educational tenet.

Fitting the School Organization to Educational Values

Several years ago a group of researchers and I initiated a series of twenty-five studies of "successful mainstreaming programs" (Biklen 1985). We invited university faculty, public school teachers, educational administrators, and parents to nominate schools or districts that they felt were achieving successful integration. We then selected a sample of these, preferring those that had been nominated multiple times and ensuring that we had representativeness: urban, suburban, and rural areas; preschool, elementary, secondary levels. The results of the study were as instructive for what they disclosed about what people called "mainstreaming" as for the specific educational practices that we observed.

The mainstreaming sites were located in a metropolitan area that included relatively small school districts of a thousand students, kindergarten through twelfth grade, as well as suburban districts of seven and eight thousand each and an urban district of over twenty thousand. Many of the organizational qualities of education in the area typified the separateness of special and regular education. All the districts complied with the U.S. mandate at the time that districts have a continuum of services available, from out-of-school placement, including institutional schooling, to regular class placements with support. Funding for special education was separate from regular education funding. All but the one urban district were empowered by state law to send students to special programs operated by a collaborative, intermediate school district.

Each district participated in helping to finance the special district, but it also had state funding. In most of the districts a special administrator supervised the special education program, distinct from the regular director of instruction or pupil services. Many had different pay scales for regular and special teachers and for such specialists as speech therapists, early childhood special educators, occupational education specialists, and physical therapists; in these, the regular teachers were paid less than the specialists. Most districts transported students with moderate and severe intellectual disabilities as well as those with physical disabilities on separate buses. Students labeled handicapped had individual education programs (IEPs); other students did not. Students without disabilities participated in annual achievement testing; students classified as disabled did not. Students without disabilities generally attended a school in their neighborhood or designated for their area; classified students attended different schools, depending on where a special education program had been established.

When we actually observed the nominated programs, we discovered that integration took three forms, only one of which can be characterized as "inclusive" schooling. We may call the three forms "teacher deals," "islands in the mainstream," and "purposeful integration."

Teacher Deals

A special education teacher believes that a student who is doing well in a special class could succeed in a typical class, perhaps with special support. The student is seen as a good prospect for integration because he or she has certain skills. The special educator approaches a regular class teacher to strike a deal. The special educator promises to consult on how the curriculum might be adapted for the classified student. The two work together, and the regular class teacher soon becomes the person responsible for the student's learning. If this teacher has not done this before, he or she may work longer hours, call friends and colleagues at night and on the weekend for advice, and learn to mainstream by doing it. The teachers who make such deals get little administrative support from the principal, district leaders, or school board. Typically, they are told, "Fine, if you think you can make it work, but it can't be at the cost of the other students." This sort of mainstreaming is common. Its success depends on the student's and teachers' ability to succeed with modest or no support.

Islands in the Mainstream

The special class or resource program that is set physically in a regular school nevertheless operates separately from the rest of the school in many ways. Often, special classes are located in one wing or at the end of a hall, away from the other classrooms. The special class teachers may report primarily to a special education administrator rather than to the building principal. The special teachers form their own team, all specialists, rather than being part of grade-level or subject-area teams. Students with disabilities interact with nondisabled students only occasionally and in limited ways, perhaps at assemblies, in the lunchroom, and during recess. The special programs may even be operated entirely by an outside authority such as an intermediate special school district that rents space in the regular school. When the overall school age population in a district increases, the special programs are sometimes moved from one building to another, to make space for the "regular" students. In some instances we observed that the special teachers had different pay schedules and vacations and in-service education days from those of the regular education staff.

This form of integration means locating students with disabilities in regular school buildings but doing little to integrate them into the school's programs. Typically, this model leads to a situation in which regular and special educators do not know one another's work very well, communication between the two groups is poor, students with disabilities become more and more estranged from the regular curriculum and their nonclassified peers, and there is a general feeling within schools that special programs are "add-ons" and therefore expendable. The drawbacks of such dual systems have been amply catalogued in the literature on mainstreaming (e.g., Biklen, 1985; Lipsky and Gartner 1989; and Stainback, Stainback, and Forest 1989).

Purposeful Integration

In an earlier publication (Biklen 1985) I called this third type "unconditional integration." But it is more appropriately labeled "purposeful," for its main quality is consciousness of intent and method. Purposeful integration moves beyond physical proximity to programmatic and social integration. Students with disabilities participate throughout the activities and spaces of the school. Integration occurs in every activity. The administrative staff has responsibility for all students; teachers and administrators collaborate in effecting classes and programs for heterogeneous groups of students, including those with the most severe and multiple disabilities and those who are most academically skilled. This approach usually involves a refashioning of classes through such approaches as team teaching, the use of teaching assistants, cooperative instruction, extensive experiential learning, parent-teacher support groups, and other similar strategies. Integration is not considered an experiment. Rather, it is a value, much like the commitment to racial equity or to teaching girls as well as boys and poor as well as rich students.

Unlike either of the other two forms, purposeful integration does not ask, "Does the student qualify for integration?" There is no test for access. Nor does the school ask, "Is integration a good idea for all students?" Integration is presumed to be preferable to segregation. As noted earlier, it is a value choice. Rather than ask *whether* to do it, the school asks *how* to do it.

As long as the organization of a school or school system reflects a dual ("special" and "regular") approach to educating students, integrationists will find themselves bending the rules, achieving "paper compliance" with the segregated model as they integrate students—in other words, interpreting the rules and regulations most liberally. An alternative approach would be for states or provinces, schools, school districts, and school boards to reorganize educational services. The process of restructuring schools from a dual to a single system would respond to a crucial shortcoming in both of the first two forms of mainstreaming. The "teacher deals" and "islands in the mainstream" approaches attempt to achieve a measure of individual integration without significantly changing the schools themselves. They do not challenge the existing organization of schools. They do not question the traditional style or content of the schools. In the dual system, special educators see themselves in an "outsider, stop gap, public relations role. . . . [Each one is] like a fix-it-all mechanic, a doctor with bandaids, a pulley (caught between competing forces), a safe haven (for the rejected student), a life preserver (for the drowning student)" (Biklen 1989, 241). The "purposeful" approach, on the other hand, assumes that before a school can effectively integrate the students, it must integrate the adults, and it must adopt inclusion as one of its main values.

Creating Purposeful Integration

Over a recent six-month period, I met monthly with a group of teachers at the Edward Smith School in Syracuse, N.Y., to talk about their work and, specifically, to discuss how they fashion their classrooms and educational approaches to students with and without disabilities. Their students included some with autism, moderate and severe retardation, emotional problems, and a variety of learning difficulties, as well as students who had no such labels. The discussions focused on classroom strategies to facilitate students' interrelationships. Predictably, the discussions also reached further.

Our group meetings became a time for consciousness-raising. Some of the teachers' questions and statements revealed the strength of the school culture to resist transformation—this was true even though this school had been involved in integration for more than ten years. Other questions suggested that a few teachers had crossed an invisible line: they had become agents of transformation, beginning with their own classrooms; they were developing a philosophy about their work that incorporated ideas similar to those of the parents who were the principal informants for this book.

During the same period when these meetings were occurring, I observed Felicia and Maria Galati at St. Basil's School in suburban Toronto, which comprises preschool through eighth grade. The school has a new principal who for two years has actively supported Maria and Felicia in typical classes. The efforts of this school and the experiences of the Galatis, their teachers, and their fellow students, as well as the reflections of the Edward Smith teachers go far toward explaining how school inclusion can work. Additional data come from visits to government (that is, public) schools in Victoria, Australia, and from examples provided by the families who were interviewed for this book.

School Leadership

St. Basil's has begun to adopt the purposeful, unconditional approach. The principal notes that the school still houses one special education class, but it will soon be gone, and the teacher will be reassigned to a homeroom, as will the students. The principal recognizes, however, that achieving integration requires more than physically relocating students. He describes the conflict between the old segregationist and the new inclusive ideology:

> There are times when a teacher says, "I can't deal with this child anymore." There is a feeling that if we could only get them [such students] assessed, we'd know what to do. But it doesn't work that way. We need something other than sending kids to the expert shop [special education]. A number of these kids upstairs [in the special class] have been there for years. That's why I've balked at placing a child in special education. We have three teacher assistants just for helping in the classroom. We're moving away from "pull out." I want teachers to say "I can do this" rather than sending them away. I always felt that the purpose of Bill 82 [Ontario's version of PL 94-142, the Education for All Handicapped Children Act] was to learn how to teach. It helps to have all kinds of books and

all kinds of activities in your classroom so kids can learn at their levels.

The principal recalls only a few incidents in which he became openly angry with teachers over the concept of unconditional inclusion. One such situation involved Felicia:

> We were struggling with Felicia in the classroom. It's particularly difficult for Felicia in teacher-directed classes such as reading and geography. Felicia would hang her head. So we sent her to other grade seven and eight classes at times to participate. When the teacher assistant and Felicia would enter another room, the teacher would say, "Oh I changed my schedule. We're not doing that [an activity] now." This happened too often. I had to call a meeting and say, "We will not do that. We are going to invite Felicia into our classes." I'm not sure people understand my thinking on this, but it hasn't happened again.

Similarly, the principal was skeptical of teachers' statements that they were not trained to work with students with disabilities. This probably meant, "Take the student away from me." He wants teachers to share his view that "there is no magic, no miracles" for teaching Felicia and Maria.

Shortly after observing St. Basil's school in Mississauga, I visited two different high schools in Victoria, Australia. At one of them, staff expressed concern that the school was unsuccessful with as many as 25 percent of the students. Predictably, these were students from lower socioeconomic backgrounds, students who were perceived as not highly motivated to participate in the academic curriculum. The teachers and administration were wringing their hands, wondering how to respond to this group, let alone to students with visible disabilities. The "integration teacher," whose job it is to promote and support the education of several students with disabilities who are being integrated into the school, reported that he was more or less alone in his efforts, forced to solicit teachers who would accept "his students" into their classes. This school could be said to be skeptical about integration, seeing it as just another in a long line of government policy impositions.

At the other high school, integration was also a new idea, yet here the principal and staff spoke proudly of their successes in retaining students from lower socioeconomic backgrounds, of attracting minority—especially aboriginal—students, of attracting "mature age" students back to school, and of their support for the integration policy. This school had initiated a broad range of community-building events such as staging dance reviews, constructing buildings on its campus (including a preschool and day-care center), and building an airplane. The school had invited a group of eight students with moderate intellectual disabilities, who were currently at a separate school, to join the student body. The principal also expressed interest in recruiting a half-dozen or more students with severe disabilities. He identified teachers and a parent leader from the board who would facilitate that process. Perhaps most revealing of the school's personality was its entrance requirements: special education teachers and teaching assistants would have to be committed to education that required a high degree of participation in expressive arts, which this happened to be this school's focus; also, students with disabilities would have to want to attend the school, as opposed to being assigned.

The two schools could not have been more different. The first wondered about the utility of keeping certain groups of students in school; it presumed that at least 25 percent were uninterested in the academic curriculum. Staff at this school felt that extensive community involvement in school projects, apprentice programs, and similar activities would be difficult to accomplish. The second school had already initiated dozens of such efforts. It had invited students from special schools to enroll at the regular school; several staff members had to spend part of their holidays in training to design integrated programs; and a parent leader had begun to establish communication with parents of children in the separate special schools. This high school brought leadership to the integration agenda.

Inclusive Events

St. Basil's initiated a schoolwide reading program in which students can win certificates and other awards for numbers of books read, and teachers dispense stickers for individual achievement. In order for the campaign to apply to all students, reading has been defined broadly. If a student writes a book, that counts as *reading* a book (the school has established a publishing center where students produce the books they write). If a student constructs a book out of pictures, that counts. If students have books read to them, those count too, as does a book viewed on film strip. Older students in the seventh and eighth grades read to younger students in the first and second grades. On the hundredth day of school, students who have read one hundred books receive commendations.

The principal at St. Basil's notes the difference between the inclusive style of education as represented by this reading campaign and the school's previous approach. "We used to have tunnel vision," he explains. "We'd say, 'This is what we teach. Jump on board if you can. All those on the periphery, you are not on board, because what we teach and the way we teach does not fit you.'"

Students as Leaders

Students with disabilities are stereotyped as being dependent. One teacher in the Edward Smith discussion group talked about developing activities that a certain student could lead: for a game of alphabetizing words, the student with disabilities initiated the game by selecting the words to be ordered. In math class a teacher engaged a group in a game involving fractions. One of these students has a severe physical disability; currently, his only means of communication are smiling or grimacing for "yes" and "no," and making selections by means of a communication device with an electronic voice. Throughout the game, each student used the communication device to announce the next person's turn. Similarly, in another game, the student with a disability operated a stopwatch to mark the times within which students were required to answer questions.

Another teacher invited a student with autism to do math problems on the chalkboard with her during a study session while other students were seated at their desks. The teacher knew that they would be impressed with their fellow student's math prowess. Casually, without any special reference to his disability, this teacher created the opportunity for them to admire that. The idea of placing students with disabilities in lead roles is not to set them apart but to create opportunities for them to fill roles that are routinely available to other students.

One of the teachers in our monthly discussion groups posed a problem that troubles many educators.

> It was always a big dilemma. You don't want this student [Adam] by himself. You don't want him going out [alone] into the community and doing all these more functional things. So you want to get typical kids involved. So you rotate typical kids. But then [I worry] I'm making that kid miss a social studies lesson. What makes it hard is . . . that it takes a while. [Sometimes] it's a whole afternoon. So that's a big issue.

These comments help explain some of the restraints teachers feel and the effects these can have on integration. First, this teacher feels constrained, presumably by the school system, to introduce the students to a certain curriculum in a more or less prescribed way and time; the teacher is seen as a transmitter of curriculum more than a creator of it. Second, the teacher's concern implies that community-based instruction is essential for students with disabilities but not for others; to the extent that nondisabled students participate, they do so primarily as companions rather than as co-learners. It suggests that learning for nondisabled students occurs best in schools; other activities may be useful socially but are tangential to the "real" business of schools. Finally, it regards school integration as a process of adapting aspects of the existing curricula, school schedules, and teacher responsibilities rather than of transforming them into something wholly new.

We can imagine a different scenario. Community-based or field instruction could become part of every student's education. In the example of Adam, his sixth-grade classmates might receive training as observers and then carry out a research project related to small store prices or consumer preferences. They might write poetry based on their observations. Or they might learn about work associated with store operations. Students might apprentice in law offices or local newspapers in jobs such as research and writing and also copying, collating, and distribution. For this and other community instruction, the "teachers" might be community experts in their fields who serve as mentors.

Back in the classroom, the teachers could create activities that bring students with severe disabilities and nondisabled students together, especially "hands on" or experiential learning projects, learning by doing.

One teacher describes her problem of how to integrate a student into a reading class when the student does not read and does not easily attend to language activities:

> Jacob doesn't do independent work. So we do "group proximity." In other words, while the other students are in English, he does daily living, fine motor kinds of skills. And I will pull my chair to his desk. We do his communication. Making choices, deciding what activity he wants to do that day. He'll point at a picture. We may do a cooking activity. We may do listening. That sort of thing. So how do I make that more a part of what we are doing in a group?

This problem is typical of those our group discussed. Jacob must be paired with other students for an activity—a classmate is assigned to help him select pictures for a scrapbook or prepare a bulletin board. Some projects naturally attract other students to participate: when Jacob's teacher was presenting the concept of communities, Jacob built a "cityscape" with cubes; other students joined him in this as they finished their reading assignments. With the teacher's encouragement, classmates also draw pictures for Jacob's communication chart. The teacher then reduces the drawings on the copier and places them on his chart.

Recently, Jacob joined a new reading group in which he works on communication separately at reading time and then joins the group at the end of the reading period to review pictures. A fellow student introduced him to the group and described his communication book to the other students. Apparently because the students have participated in constructing the book, they feel some pride in it. Unless group activities are carefully orchestrated, an adult must be with Jacob at all times to help keep him focused and to prevent him from placing objects in his mouth. If the students put on a play related to their reading, Jacob can participate in the preparations and even the performance. Or Jacob and his classmates collect pictures to create collages that portray scenes from the books. The class is now reading Roald Dahl's *James and the Giant Peach* (1962). This may engender an activity with peaches—for example, cooking with peaches—in which Jacob can have a central part.

At the secondary level, in the same school district, students are also often paired in course activities. Those who do not have disabilities may volunteer their study hall time or free periods to accompany a student with a severe disability in an integrated class. Paired students may also participate together in computer instruction, weight lifting, jogging, or jobs in the school. Students who do not have disabilities are also recruited to facilitate the involvement of students with disabilities in after-school extracurricular activities. In Ontario particularly, through the work of Marsha Forest (1987), students are recruited for "Circles of Friends" to support students with disabilities, as was done for Catherine Woronko. Felicia enjoyed this same kind of support at St. Basil's. Fellow students joined her in certain classes, at the lunch hour, and in walking from one class to another. Similarly, in the schools of Woodstock, New Brunswick, Canada, students are often paired in classrooms. Thus, for example, I observed a student with a moderate intellectual disability working with two nondisabled students in a regular biology laboratory class. Although her participation in the group was partial—she could not prepare written descriptions of dissections as well as the other students might—she helped to do the actual dissections and to prepare slides for the microscope. She could also examine the slides and could accompany her peers on field explorations to collect materials for microscope viewing.

Teachers as Models

Two of the teachers in our discussion group collaborated with me in writing a chapter for an edited book (Biklen, Corrigan, and

Quick 1989). In "Beyond Obligation" we explored strategies for promoting positive relations between students. The teachers had a treasure of ideas. One set up a question-and-answer box into which students could place any questions. From time to time, the teacher herself "would 'plant' notes that would ask: 'Why does Sheila . . . bite herself and other people?'" By asking such questions, the teacher gave herself a natural context for airing issues that were on students' minds.

The most central form of modeling by teachers for students concerned communication. These teachers follow several key principles: speak directly to the student with a disability as you would to any student in an instructional situation; assume that the student understands what you are communicating, even if you cannot be sure that he or she does; establish eye contact with the student; speak in a normal style and tone of voice, avoiding excessive joking and a high-pitched or singsong voice; do not draw attention to disability-related behaviors such as drooling but offer to wipe a student's chin or and give other assistance in a matter-of-fact way; seize on opportunities to be self-disclosing or less than perfect yourself so as to make it clear to students that it is all right to make mistakes; and above all, avoid being too effusive with praise or patronizing in other ways. These are all specific, unobtrusive skills of interaction that the other students can observe and learn.

When a student was particularly upset, these teachers talked out loud about what might be troubling him or her. This gave the others a chance to try to interpret their fellow student's behavior and freed them from feeling that they had to define a classmate as bad; they could begin to think of the behavior as separate from the person, as something a person *does* rather than what the person *is*. Eventually, the students began to interpret such behavior on their own. One student explained to her teacher, "Marissa is really upset because she can't find her snack." Another remarked, "Eric really wants to do that too," and "Eric needs to be moved. He's been in that position for a long time, and he's uncomfortable."

As one teaching assistant explained, they were even able to step back from difficult situations and remain interpretive. By the time she got outside at recess one day, Andy had bitten several students. They went to the school nurse, who said they were all right, despite the bite marks. "But the kids were all sticking up for Andy. They told me that he just felt caged in and frustrated when he found himself in a tight group of them." This was a particularly interesting response because the students not only interpreted Andy's behavior but interpreted their own part in it. They presumed that if they changed their behavior, Andy might change his: if they did not crowd him, he would not become excited, anxious, or frustrated. The teachers had modeled an interpretive process, and the students had adopted it as their own.

In the book *Gentle Teaching*, John McGee and his colleagues explain that teaching people not to be self-abusive or abusive to other people depends on a certain approach to difficult behavior: Caregivers [teachers, friends, relatives] need to reflect on and actualize a posture that brings full acceptance of the humanity of the person, in spite of oftentimes repulsive behaviors. This means cultivating a true solidarity with the person. . . . This posture is at the core of gentle teaching" (McGee, Menousek, and Hobbs 1987, 156).

One of the teachers in our monthly discussion group exemplifies this outlook or "posture." We can see it in her explanation of how she approaches a student's self-abuse or tantrums:

> Fighting, scratching, kicking! I really feel strongly about not removing kids from the classroom when that is happening, for a variety of reasons. One of them is that the kid may be *trying* to get out of the class. Another is that it is important for the other students to see how you process through with it, when the child is upset. In such a situation, it is important to express aloud the feelings that the student may be experiencing, so that the other students can see how you the teacher are interpreting the episode.

It might seem easier to remove the student from the classroom and off center stage, but in fact, such events are learning experiences. A consulting teacher expresses the same philosophy in regard to a sixth-grade girl and a fifth-grade boy:

> [When] kids [are] hurting each other, we have a tendency to deal with it by taking a kid off . . . to get control before we

can bring them back and be with kids. With Janine, I think just the opposite is true. When we put her with other kids, that gave her a reason to act well . . . something to keep her mind on. And with Bob Cross, I think the same thing is true. When he is with other kids, he has something to focus on. Very often it is the being with other kids that is the focus, or playing a game. Usually his behavior is better [under those circumstances]. So it is just the reverse . . . of doing . . . skill building first [before letting him be with other students]. Socialization is an end in itself for him. It has its own motivation.

Of course, not all teacher modeling concerns difficult behavior. Maria Galati's teachers talk loudly enough to her that classmates can pick up ways to interact with her. They talk to Maria as they would to another student, presuming her competence. Maria does not speak, and she does not have signs for "yes" and "no," but the other students can tell by her smiles when she enjoys something such as a piece of music or being wheeled quickly in her chair. The teachers emphasize the importance of supporting Maria's head and neck; at the same time they avoid casting Maria in the role of a fragile doll. Students are encouraged to transfer her from her wheelchair to a mat, or to a hammock in the classroom; classmates sit in the hammock with her. Once, the teaching assistant noted, "I turned around and Maria was in the cot. They didn't ask, they did it. You see some of the children know Maria in the neighborhood, and they apparently move her around at home. So they didn't think anything of it."

On the way home from school one day, Maria's wheelchair tipped over, and she got a broken nose. Her neighborhood friend, who was pushing the chair, naturally felt bad and blamed herself. But Rose Galati understood that it was important for this girl as well as other students not to become afraid of Maria's disabilities as a result of the accident. She told the student that she didn't blame her and invited the friend and other children to the house the same day to bake cookies. This allowed them to see for themselves that Maria was going to be all right.

Teachers hope that the structure and group activities they develop will lead students to initiate interactions on their own. During homeroom, for example, Andy was just sitting at his desk when another student said, "Come on, lets write on the board." His teacher comments, "I never thought that would happen unless I was always there creating the situation. But I can see it's important to let them be once in a while and see what happens." Many teachers talk to students about what it means to support each other; the importance of looking to the person being helped for guidance on whether help is needed, how much, and how it is best given; and the value of being able to take criticism. One student wrote in her journal about the things she does with a student who has a severe disability, wondering if she does too much, if she is "taking over" rather than merely being supportive. In another instance, a student with autism reached out and hit his teacher's arm. A fellow student came up to him and scolded, "You're not ready to go to music yet. I think you should sit down until you are ready." Was this student merely applying pressure to a fellow student? Or was she taking on an adult role, becoming his "teacher" and thereby diminishing the status of her classmate? Her action seemed to border on both; it would be important in such a situation to encourage the class to talk about and discover ways of expressing support that enhance a person's status or at least do not detract from it.

Occasionally, having learned from teachers' examples, students themselves will set the standard for giving assistance. Such was the case when one student told her teacher that she was being too protective: "I leaned over to Jane," reports the teacher, "because Marissa was next to her, and said she should show Marissa how to get through the row and up to the stage. Then I started to get up myself, and one of the kids turned around and said, 'Mrs. Quick, sit down. She knows what she is doing.' I was sort of set aback, in a good way. I felt good about that. Sure enough Marissa did get through and up to the stage" (Biklen, Corrigan, and Quick 1989, 219).

Making It Natural

In another classroom, the teacher became concerned that Sam was being left out at lunchtime. "I don't know if it was his behavior, but we had kids who did not want to have anything to do with him. It got so bad that we had a class meeting about it." The class talked about the importance of having *everyone* feel part of the class. The teacher suggested that the students form into groups for lunch, thus ensuring that no one would be alone. She explained how the students responded: "After a month the kids were saying, 'We don't need a system. We'll make sure he's okay.' They were volunteering. It was great to see that. They were starting to see him as a person and not 'Oh we have to sit at the table with him.' It comes and goes, but there are a few kids who without having to be pushed want to be with him now."

The teacher was able to use this situation to address other issues of relations between students. "It was not as if Sam was the only one having problems. There was a lot of general meanness and isolation going on. It wasn't like everybody else was doing great and Sam's was the only problem." So the teacher focused first on Sam and how Sam might feel:

> "Do you think because when you talk to Sam and he doesn't respond that he doesn't understand?" [she asked the class]. I think some of them thought that because he doesn't respond, he doesn't understand, and they can say anything they want in front of him. So we had to get it across . . . that he does understand. Then, from talking about that, it went on to the whole class discussing how we are not being nice to each other.

This teacher concluded her description of the situation with a self-critique: "It probably would have been nicer to do a whole class [discussion] and then put Sam in more 'subtly.' We were lucky that it evolved the way it did naturally."

Another teacher expanded on this theme, also arguing for classroom discussions that do not give undue attention to disabilities:

> There may be a lot of kids who feel ostracized or who just feel they don't have the skills to get involved in a dance or after-school activity, for whatever reason. There are so many reasons why a student may be socially ostracized that it wouldn't make sense just to pick a child because he is disabled. So this kind of

activity can be supportive for all the kids; the idea . . . [is] that we all want to become more involved in the activities of the school.

These teachers talked among themselves to discover new approaches to their work. They sorted out ways of addressing issues of difference and acceptance; they searched for an approach that could account for the feelings and needs of students with disabilities in a way that recognizes that other students share these concerns.

A fourth-grade teacher had a situation nearly opposite to the one of students being left out. Her class had come to recognize that while one of the students with a disability had a difficult time initiating social interactions, she liked to read. Consequently, some of the students started to leave little notes on her desk. These were a way for students to reach out and include their classmate. The teacher, however, became concerned that the student's desk was becoming especially messy and that only this one student was on the receiving end of the note-sending activity. The teacher decided to incorporate the students' note- and letter-writing into the curriculum. Handing out paper to all the students, she explained anyone could write a note to anyone else so long as the writer signed it and said in the note only things that he or she would be willing to say in person. In other words, students were encouraged to be sensitive to each other. They could write during one free time in the morning and during snack time. Tammy, the student who had received the original notes, would come into the class and regularly ask, "Did I get any messages today?" Thus, an activity that she enjoyed and that capitalized on a skill she had became a natural classroom activity. When Tammy did not receive a note, the teacher seized the opportunity to encourage her to write notes to other people. In describing this activity to a group of other teachers, she remarked: "Even if a student could not write but could draw, other students could draw back."

In a first-grade classroom two teachers implemented a system of partners. The plan grew out of their observation that one student with a disability would initiate interactions with other students by approaching them and squeezing their arms. The teachers announced the idea of forming partners as a classwide practice. Students were asked to select partners, either by placing a hand on another's shoulder (that is, touching, not squeezing) or by saying something. One of the teachers explained how she guaranteed that the students with disabilities would be included: "The order of picking kids was really important. We made sure that the 'special' kids were picked toward the beginning so that they wouldn't be left sitting there unpicked. In other words, we structured how kids picked each other. But now the other kids are doing it. I don't have to do it. This worked because they had been picked by a special kid and had gotten comfortable with it." This classroom holds meetings in which students are encouraged to talk about their feelings, the activities they like and why. The teachers also observe the children on the playground and then talk to them about what they observe.

Grouping for Inclusion

Research has found that just placing students with and without disabilities in physical proximity helps them all develop improved attitudes toward one another (Towfighy-Hooshyar and Zingle, 1984). If students are supported and encouraged to interact, these attitudes and their willingness to initiate interactions improve (Voeltz 1982 and 1984). The teachers in our discussion group talked about how they use physical proximity and consciously group students to spur interaction and acceptance. As one teacher explained: "There are times when we group specifically to put kids with their friends. Sometimes when we put them with new kids, we try to have it be in an activity where we know the special-needs child is going to be successful. The point of it is for them to get to know each other."

In many classrooms, students' desks are organized in clusters, four or six together facing inward, rather than in rows. This facilitates group projects and general sharing of work. One teacher used seating as an instructional tool, applying it for reasons of both academic instruction and social support:

I change the regular seating chart fairly often. I put any active kid nearer me. When we break into groups, I put a low speller, a medium speller, and a high speller together. It's good to shift around enough so that there is not a special responsibility for any student. As well, you want to make sure you don't switch students around so much that it's confusing. By January I'm on the fourth seating chart. No one stays in the same place.

Often, the teacher breaks up best friends, knowing that students are more willing to engage another student, particularly one they do not know, if they are not with a best friend—and, she jokingly noted, "they might pay more attention too." In other words, seating can help students expand their relationships in the classroom and support learning.

The ability to be part of a small group is a crucial skill for many situations, not the least of which is being in large groups such as in the cafeteria at lunchtime or in school assemblies. One teacher explained, "In the cafeteria, you don't survive because you know how to be part of that large group. You survive because you have a smallish group that you can focus on." Teachers in the classrooms try to prepare students for these situations. For example, a teacher noted that one of her students focuses on his work and does not lapse into tantrums or get up from his seat if she is with him. She is trying to remove herself from that immediate support role, helping the student to become less dependent on adults: "I'm trying to get away from direct support by placing a student between me and Ibrahim. Now he'll stay [in place] if you can get him to focus on the kid next to him." One teacher calls this "positioning": deciding where to sit, trying to move away from direct support by helping students develop the skill to find support or a sense of security with fellow students.

The effectiveness of any grouping or positioning depends on a number of factors, including the students' level of skill in independence and communication, their comfort with one another, and the nature of the joint or group project. The teachers felt that group projects and class projects—for example, a weekend of camping out—were particularly good community- and communication-building activities for the beginning part of the school year.

Getting Out of Students' Way

As the Edward Smith group met month after month, talking about student relationships, we found that the ideas we shared all required a common approach. Teachers saw themselves as creating the conditions in which students would interact. One called it "making opportunities" for interaction: how can we create situations where students will interact, come to know one another, and then be mutually supportive? And can we do it naturally, without letting the structure dominate to such an extent that students would need that structure in order to repeat the skill of interaction later, on their own? As we have noted, experiential learning and group activities were favored strategies. In addition, the teachers needed to judge when they could and should remove themselves from class interactions and allow the students to develop their own relations. For example, if a student saw a classmate communicate with a sign that she wanted to go to the bathroom or that she wanted to use a communication device, the teacher could say, "Oh, well, why don't you go with her?" or "Why don't you help her?" Thus the teacher would not become the funnel through which all interactions with a student with disabilities must flow. She can encourage students to interact, encourage them to engage fellow students without ever explicitly saying she is doing that. She can help them to adopt such interaction as natural and to see their classmate as someone to whom they can respond directly, not as the teacher's special property.

Maria Galati's teachers do this. Walking down the hall of the school, her teachers encourage other students to push Maria's wheelchair. And of course for certain classes and times of day—physical education, recess, lunch—students literally take over the support of Felicia and Maria, walking them around the playground, restyling their hair, playing music, helping Felicia change for gym, and concocting adapted physical education activities.

Such student interactions have become increasingly common as Felicia and Maria follow course schedules similar to those of other students. Felicia's schedule includes art, gym, family studies (a life skills curriculum with cooking and sewing), computers, and religion. During academic classes such as reading or math, Felicia works with her aide and often another student to prepare elaborate bulletin board displays. Other students contribute materials for the bulletin boards. Felicia needs to be assisted, with a helper's hands over her own, for every aspect of the bulletin board preparation, but she appears to enjoy the color and physical activity of constructing the displays. Felicia moans and hangs her head down when she is bored, whereas she smiles, flaps her hands, and (if she is sitting) stomps her feet when she is happy or excited.

It appears that as students learn the skills of interacting and come to appreciate each other, they also learn that it is important to talk about relationships and interdependence. At Edward Smith, a new student joined an upper elementary grade at midyear. Nancy, who has Down syndrome, was feeling alone and friendless; in the lunchroom she would sit by herself, not talking to other students, and each night she would cry about being left out. Being aware of the problem, one of the teachers seized an opportunity in class one day to call to her attention the fact that a student had just shown her friendship by expressing an interest in doing an activity with her. Another student who heard the teacher's remark conducted a class meeting of her own: "I was in the back of the class and I was calling this act of friendship to Nancy's attention," the teacher remembers. "All of a sudden I had someone in the middle of the class standing up and saying, 'Whoever is Nancy's friend, put up your hand.'" The hands shot up; the group expressed their friendship to Nancy and at the same time became conscious of her feeling left out. They announced their resolve to change that.

If the teacher had orchestrated this discussion directly, the students probably would have viewed it differently. But this was not an instance of a teacher lecturing students on how they should behave. The students lectured each other. It was more like a pep rally than a scolding or advice session. And because they created it on their terms, they probably felt more ownership for the message being communicated. They were feeling and showing their responsibility.

Progress Notes

When Mary Lou Accetta's son Melvin first arrived at the Jowonio school, he had only a couple of signs, and to many people even these were unintelligible. As one teacher remembers, "We thought he had no language abilities." But he quickly developed more signs. Today, in the public schools, his language has blossomed to the point where he no longer uses signs and instead speaks with assurance; Mary Lou estimates that 90 percent of what he says can be understood by his classmates. He used to run off when he was supposed to go to a specific location; now he can walk independently. There is multiple significance in such changes: they give us encouragement for the educational process and announce its importance; they reaffirm the notion that all people are capable of development; and they speak to Melvin's own personal growth.

Charting or accounting for students' progress is a crucial element in the inclusion process and probably the one best way to communicate the importance of education and of the individual student. When we are able to see change, of whatever magnitude, we have reason for optimism. Recently, when a teacher noted that a student named Jarod was able to walk independently downstairs to one of his classes and go to the bathroom on his own (as long as the hallway was empty of other students), one of his former teachers expressed amazement: "That's incredible. We'd have to have an adult walking toward him and someone on the other end sending him." Another teacher reported that a student named Samir no longer runs from the school building. Now that he attends middle school where part of his academic program is working in the community, he has stopped "running."

Often, it is classmates who mark a student's progress. Kaisha entered the school knowing only two sentences: "Go bathroom" and "Water please." Several years later she speaks volumes, although usually in sentences that she has heard others say. She also reads, often looking up to see if other students are watching her demonstrate her ability. Observing this, several students have expressed surprise: "Is Kaisha really reading? I didn't know she could do that." This and other modest events become causes for taking stock. Max, a student classified as autistic, is quite academically but not socially skilled. One of his teachers described him as "one of the highest functioning autistic kids the school has seen." Recently, Max heard his classmates using the phrase "Oh yeah, oh yeah," as if to say "Right" or "Great." Later, several students heard Max repeating the phrase himself, saying "Oh yeah, oh yeah" and laughing. This caused one student to remark, "Max laughed. Hey, I remember when Max laughed in fourth grade."

Rules of Accommodation

It would be naive and insensitive to assume that "treating students with disabilities like anyone else" will make all students feel or be part of their school community. Some students will not have the skills to make friends or even to enter discussions. Those who do not have disabilities may lack the skills to interact with a student who does not speak. Some students may need course materials in large print, in braille, or on tape. Another may need a phonic ear to amplify the voices of teachers and classmates. In other words, students don't all need the *same* treatment; some need accommodations.

One standard for deciding how much accommodation is necessary is this: *What will enable a student to participate in a way that is similar to or the same as the participation of other students?* Anything less compromises the student's education. Adrienne Asch provides an excellent example of this principle in discussing the Supreme Court's handling of Amy Rowley's need for interpreter services. Essentially, the court ruled that her right was not to educational opportunity commensurate with that available to her nondisabled peers but only to a program of "some educational benefit." Hence, since she was earning passing grades, she did not need an interpreter, even though she could understand—by lipreading—little more than half of what her teachers said. "If students are to develop the ability to sift out the essential from the illustrative in a lecture, they must themselves have the full text of that lecture communicated to them," Asch argues. Similarly, "if they are to join in class discussions, they must know what other students have said." An interpreter's account of students' and teachers' every word would place Amy Rowley "on a par with the rest of the group for knowing all that is going on in the group." Interpreters would give Amy an "equal chance at classroom life" (Asch 1989, 186).

On the other hand, some adaptations can actually exclude a student from full participation: a student being transported to and from school on a separate bus, a student becoming isolated from others in the class because he or she is constantly in the presence of a teaching aide (an aide may unintentionally become a chaperon or the person's only companion), or a student being taken out of class for speech therapy sessions just at the most exciting part of the class period—for example, when students are competing in math games or other joint projects. Nondisabled students commonly observe these kinds of discriminatory treatment and do not know how or if they can do anything to change it.

Marsha Forest has devised ways of involving students in consciousness-raising about such conditions and in changing them by inventing their own accommodations. The methods follow two principles: first, *take the perspective of students,* and second, *accommodate only as far as is necessary.* Forest describes two methods she developed at McGill University: "Circles of Friends" and MAPS (McGill Action Planning System). Both are strategies whereby students and schools may examine and nurture participation by students with disabilities in their classrooms, with other students, and throughout their schools (Forest 1987).

"Circles of Friends" has two meanings. It refers first to establishing a support group of classmates who become allies of a student with severe disabilities. They go to class with the student; they do things together after school and on weekends. They are a group. "Circles of Friends" also refers to the process of drawing concentric circles on a piece of paper to indicate the various people who spend time with a person, from family and relatives in the inner circle, to best friends in the next, to acquaintances, to those people who are employed to be of assistance (for example, the doctor, dentist, "personal care attendant," and speech therapist or some other specialist). This process often reveals that some people have few friends in their lives beyond immediate family and people paid to spend time with them.

MAPS incorporates some of the characteristics of traditional individual education planning but rejects others. It involves parents, teachers, and administrators, as well as a student's friends or support group, in the planning sessions. A facilitator convenes the entire group to review information about a student's involvement in school life and to find ways to reduce any isolation that he or she may be experiencing. Only those people who know the student well may contribute to the discussion; technical or more professionally derived information is given less significance than are observations and interpretations. Of course, this reverses the usual emphasis of traditional case planning conferences. Professional jargon has no place in MAPS. The group examines the student's strengths and needs, but it does not speak of weaknesses and deficits; instead, it adopts a tone of optimism and mutual support.

The MAPS facilitator asks the assembled group—the student and his or her parents, siblings, friends, teachers, and principal—to state their "most favorite vision" of the student's future. Participants are encouraged to "dream a little" and to ignore concerns about funding, government rules, and other perceived limitations. Classmates, for example, might envision a student with a severe disability in his or her adult years living in a supported apartment, holding down a job, having a circle of friends, enjoying going to the movies with friends, or continuing an emerging interest in art or dance. Once "dreams" have been articulated, the group shares "worst fears" for the student; these might include such unhappy outcomes as being alone or institutionalized, sitting in an empty room, bored, and not learning. By focusing on fears, the group reminds itself of the importance of building relationships with the student.

The third phase of MAPS planning involves generating a list of qualities that describe the student, always emphasizing the positive, and identifying the student's interests and needs. The list may include such words as strong, spontaneous, energetic, funny, creative, quick, curious, attractive, bossy, fearless, and friendly. In one session a principal described the student as an excellent "greeter," and a "good will ambassador": "She greets people really well. She can walk right up to people and say "'Hi, how are you?' . . . not much after that, but she is good at that." A fellow student noted, "She needs more contact with boys." Another thought she needed more opportunities to be in conversations. Her mother spoke of her need to have a broader social circle of people who care about her and who are interested in spending time with her. Her father encouraged a focus on building her self-confidence. He believes she'd like to learn to do more things for herself, such as turning a tape recorder on and off. A teacher would like to have her become more autonomous, able to ride a bus, for example. And the principal thought she needed more cooperation from people around her.

The MAPS approach concludes with the group strategizing together about what a week would look like for the student. In practical terms, this provides a framework for fellow students, parents, and teachers to become the student's allies. In the example cited above, fellow students suggested that she come to school on a city bus, as they do, instead of by taxi. They offered to assist her when necessary. The students also recommended that she join them in a typical homeroom class. Since this student is already participating independently in a typical, integrated dance class, she will probably want to continue that. Her teacher recommended that one period a day be spent on community-referenced instruction. Because the MAPS process involves friends and supporters strategizing together about a peer's strengths and interests, the group becomes a social change alliance more than a diagnostic and placement meeting. It is an open process that generates ideas *and* creates a supportive community around the student. It looks beyond bureaucratic constraints, recognizes the relationship of a person's isolation to social conditions, and does not view the disabled person as a deficit-ridden problem. The students become one another's allies.

When our monthly group of teachers met to talk about these methods, there was both enthusiasm and concern. One teacher wanted everyone else to see a video about Circles of Friends: "When I saw that video . . . there was the family [in the inner circle], then a blank circle and a blank circle and then the circle with people you pay to be with the person. That was very powerful for me." The circles format helped him see how isolated some students can be. Perhaps more important, he related the problem of no or limited friendships to the school. "I would like all of us to see it [the video] because that's the thing about . . . us being with the kids too much. It just really struck me, 'Get out of the kids' way so that they can make friends.'" As this teacher quickly noted, however, "just getting out of the way" will not by itself create friendships or even participation for a student.

At the same time, many of the teachers were not entirely comfortable with either the MAPS or the Circles approach. They asked, "Won't they [these methods] call attention to the kids with disabilities?" One teacher said, "I have this pit in my stomach [worrying] that she wouldn't have anybody in the inner circles." The teachers decided that they would be comfortable with something like MAPS only if they used it for several students in a class and not just one student who has a disability. It might be useful as a structure for getting students to know and spend time with one another, like forming the class into groups for the lunch period so that no students were left out, but ultimately, the teachers wanted more natural relationships and support to form. Similarly, they weren't sure they'd be comfortable using the Circles exercise with students; they were afraid it could become hurtful unless they could find a way to make it private for each student.

Rose Galati points out that though such concerns may be valid, as children enter adolescence a student with severe or multiple disabilities can easily be left outside of various self-selecting groups of students. She believes that the Circles of Friends concept as well as MAPS can help nondisabled students understand that for students with severe disabilities friendship can have a different meaning than it has for other students. She notes that unlike other students, her daughters cannot initiate friendships—for example, they cannot call up classmates or speak with them—and consequently, they cannot easily participate in either the letting-go of friends or the pursuit of them. They have to depend on their peers to understand that fact, and Rose views the Circles and MAPS techniques as structured ways of enabling fellow students to do so. Forest recommends using these methods when a student first enters a program as a way of helping him or her achieve connections with other students, and also at times of crisis when a student may be ignored or left out. She too worries that the Circles and MAPS techniques may become routinized in schools and possibly detract from teachers' and students' efforts to develop more natural forms of support and friendship.

Schools That Learn

In the past when the idea of integration has been suggested for so-called "able-bodied only" or "typical" schools, some teachers have resisted it on the grounds of inadequate training. (We noted earlier that such statements often mask an unwillingness to teach students with disabilities.) Not surprisingly, the schools that have demonstrated an openness to integration generally are open schools in which the following practices are common: teachers regularly share ideas about curricula, classroom organization, and other issues; parents routinely come to the school, participate in meetings, and talk with administrators and teachers about the students and programs; the school encourages and initiates involvement of the outside community in school programs; visitors are welcome to observe throughout the school and its classrooms; teachers and administrators regularly visit other schools to gather new ideas. The open schools seem to operate on the principle that to integrate students, a school must first integrate its adults: specialist teachers and subject-area or grade-level teachers must collaborate.

Parent Participation

Although it is rarely articulated as a principle of school operation or governance, schools that effectively include students with disabilities typically elicit significant parent participation. At the Jowonio school, for example, the first integrated school that Ben

Lehr attended, parents serve on teacher-hiring committees, on fund-raising committees, on parent-teacher task forces that provide training for other schools in the inclusion approach, as volunteers in classrooms, and as regular informants to teachers about children's activities and abilities at home. At the Edward Smith school, parents participate in parent-teacher support groups where they talk about the progress of inclusive education, in pot-luck dinners for parents and teachers and the children themselves, and in the parent-teacher organization. As at Jowonio, they also serve on delegations to spread information about inclusive education to other schools, educational groups, and community groups. Among the methods of parent inclusion that are observable at these and other schools are the following: parents observing in classrooms; parents as teaching assistants; parent-teacher discussion groups; parent-teacher organizations; parent-teacher-administrator program planning committees; individual educational program planning groups; school management committees; social events; booster clubs (that is, as fund-raising and event organizers); notebooks passed between parents and teachers about student progress; parent narratives of student experiences, abilities, and interests; and parent-teacher phone conversations.

Inclusive, Effective Education

Constant Inclusion

Reading Nora Groce's book (1985) about deafness on Martha's Vineyard, an island off the coast of Massachusetts, one has the feeling of walking into unreality. Groce describes her drives around the island with an elderly lifetime resident, Gale Huntington. He recounts for her who lived where, the nature of their work, who their relations were, the extent of their wealth, and what people thought of them. It wasn't long before she began to realize that a seemingly large number of the Vineyard residents had been deaf, though Huntington would mention the fact almost as an afterthought: "Come to think of it," he would say, "he was deaf and dumb too."

By Huntington's recollection, deaf islanders were common into the early twentieth century. But when Nora Groce asked one woman in her eighties about people "who were handicapped by deafness," the woman declared, "Oh, those people weren't handicapped. They were just deaf."

It is difficult to read this comment without wondering if the woman was not camouflaging the fact that people had very serious disabilities. But as Groce continued her inquiry, she found much that verified the elders' attitude. People who were profoundly deaf and unspeaking were married to hearing people. People who were deaf held the same range of jobs in the community as hearing people. Although most of the deaf were middle class, one man was reputed to be among the wealthiest people on the island. Apparently most people thought of deafness in the same way that Huntington and the eighty-year-old woman did—as so unremarkable that it was barely worth mentioning. It was certainly not regarded as cause for calling someone handicapped.

In today's society, deafness ranks as a serious disability and usually as a handicap. People who are deaf encounter significant discrimination in employment, in schooling, and in social relations; they are often socially excluded from the hearing world and forced into the deaf community psychologically and often physically as well. The title of sociologist Paul Higgins's book, *Outsiders in a Hearing World* (1982), makes this very point. In Martha's Vineyard, on the other hand, people who were deaf did not apparently congregate; in fact, if a deaf person had called a meeting only of other deaf people, a large number of hearing people—including many of the person's closest friends—would not have understood and would have felt excluded. In the island culture, it did not make sense to organize people on the basis of disability. Town records often did not make note of whether a person was hearing or not.

Several factors appear to have influenced perceptions of deafness on Martha's Vineyard. The incidence of hearing impairment was high—approximately 1 in 150 persons island-wide. But in some areas the proportion was far greater: in one town the ratio was 1 to 49, in another 1 to 25, and in one neighborhood of one town it was 1 in 4 (Groce 1985, 42). Deafness reached into most families. Groce's title discloses the most important reason why deafness did not achieve the status of a handicap: *Everyone Here Spoke Sign Language*. People who were deaf could go to a meeting in which a hearing person was speaking and count on numerous hearing participants to translate. Deaf and hearing people could marry, work together, go to school together, and communicate freely. Universal signing averted the disenfranchisement that so typically characterizes the relations of deaf people to the hearing world.

Finally, and perhaps as important as the signing, people who were deaf were *never* segregated from the mainstream society. In fact, in the experiences of people who were deaf in eighteenth- and nineteenth-century Martha's Vineyard, the term "integration" would have been as foreign a concept as the term "handicap." Put another way, membership in mainstream society was constant, for both hearing and nonhearing people.

This suggests a principle for schooling. Linda Till mentioned it when she described what she wants for her daughter Becky at home and in school: full participation in every aspect of family and school life. She understands that the moment students with disabilities are removed from regular environments and separated from other students—whether for classes, homeroom, transportation, extracurricular activities, or social events—they become outsiders. Even if they are often integrated for particular activities such as art, music, and gym, their role is as outsiders being "let in" or "invited" for prescribed events. Typically, they are let in if they can meet certain criteria for behavior, performance of certain skills, and so forth; in short, their participation becomes conditional. Linda Till wants something more like the situation Groce describes on Martha's Vineyard, where participation was expected, indeed assumed. Under Vineyard conditions, the school would adapt to the student's communication or other styles or characteristics without seizing on them as justification for exclusion and discrimination. Making modifications that permit full participation would be everyone's work, not the sole province of specialists. Students would have access to a very broad range of school experiences and would presumably not be excluded from any.

The Effective, Inclusive School

Aside from the implication that regular classes belong to students without disabilities, concern for the consequences of integrated schooling on all students is reasonable. Our observations of classrooms and schools suggest that inclusion is not burdensome; in fact, inclusion requires many of the same features as any quality schooling.

Commitment

The educational community shares a democratic philosophy, purpose, and values about education. The school espouses a commitment to every student's learning. The school defines excellence in such a way that every student can aspire to it.

There is a sense of community about the purpose. Parents, teachers, administrators, students, and the public collaborate in formulating what they believe and what they want to achieve through schooling. In other words, the authority of the school evolves democratically from the people involved in the community of the school.

All school leaders—principals, superintendents, board members, and others—assume responsibility for the success of the inclusion.

Organizational Framework

The organization and procedures (including financing) of the school reflect its philosophy, values, and purposes. This includes a single administrative structure for developing the educational programs of all students.

School policies reflect the school mission. For example, policies about student admissions (all students in a geographic area; any students within a section of the city or town) apply equally to all students, irrespective of abilities.

Teachers and specialists collaborate in the development of classes and programs for the full range of students. Teachers participate in group problem-solving. Specialist teachers and other staff participate in subject-area or grade-level teams. In other words, the adults are integrated.

Elements of Schooling

Students are grouped across ability levels. Students of varying abilities work collaboratively as coparticipants on educational projects. The school uses educational strategies such as cooperative learning to foster learning by mixed ability groups.

The school ensures opportunities for all students to participate in the full range of educational activities.

The school incorporates learning-by-doing or experiential learning into all areas of the curricula.

Teachers model social skills and educational approaches: for example, how to communicate with a student using a communication board; how to interpret what might have caused a student to become upset (rather than attaching blame); how to support a student.

The school provides frequent opportunities for students to receive comments (rewards and criticisms) about their performance.

Accommodations for students' disabilities are introduced only as necessary. They are accomplished *naturally* and unobtrusively within classes, programs, and schools so as to minimize the identification of a student who has a disability as significantly different from other students. In other words, the school uses strategies that enable a student with a disability to participate in a way that is similar to or the same as that of other students.

Teachers create opportunities for students with disabilities, like other students, to fill leadership roles in their classes and school.

Teaching and the school atmosphere maximize independence with minimum supervision yet recognize natural interdependence. Teachers avoid getting in the way of students' getting to know each other.

Students learn how to support each other, to appreciate each other's needs, and to be friends.

The school evaluates programs for their effectiveness in integrating students across ability levels. Educators revise instructional approaches on the basis of evaluation findings.

Consulting teachers assist in observing students in their classrooms and in developing curricula and suggestions on troublesome situations.

The educational community sets high expectations for students, based on knowledge of their skills and school program.

The school uses a common language for describing students, curriculum content, classes, teachers, and other aspects of schooling; in other words, it abandons much of the medical and psychological language that permeates the field of special education: for example, "diagnostic prescriptive teaching" and "clinical intervention," as well as such broad and generally uninformative labels for students as "neurologically impaired," "learning disabled," "mentally retarded," and "emotionally disturbed."

Teachers, parents, and students recognize one another as critical thinkers, capable of formulating curricula and school environment.

Ideology and Social Policy

In her book *Of Such Small Differences,* Joanne Greenberg portrays her sense of what happens when sighted and hearing people relate to people who are both deaf and blind. It is a classic clash of cultures, one dominant over the other. John, the book's protagonist, is "deaf-blind." He works at a sheltered workshop, has a rehabilitation counselor, and writes poetry. The workshop director encourages him to create poetry to sell, the kind that can be printed on cards and posters and sold as the product of a deaf-blind poet. He does so, and the poetry is ordinary, describing, for example, love as an ocean or as giving one wings to soar over a vast expanse. When John asks his hearing and sighted lover if she likes the poem, she grants that "it is nice," but "it is not your poem" (Greenberg 1988, 115). Though her response disappoints him, it is honest and sensitive: The poem's imagery is drawn not from his world but from the sighted, hearing world. *His* poetry would sound different, convey a different experience, disclose how *he* knows his world.

Writing out of his experience, he says of his cat, Forebuds: "Unfolded, Forebuds is swimming my leg." He writes about a gated iron fence that he passes each day in the city, near his house. He portrays the fence as walking the block with him, the iron posts like spires, perhaps weapons for soldiers. Since the fence and gate are near his home, their feel marks the end of his journey, a welcoming back. Over the years he has continually been surprised as familiar landmarks pass away, succumbing to "development." He worries that this may be the future fate of his favored gate, wondering if its owner will "carry it away and leave me friendless and without a fantasy in my geography." Of course, John must write again of the "ocean." This time he imagines it a "monster beating slowly," the water its "pulsing blood," its uneven waves like the push and pull of a "sighted guide in traffic," its wind like ten winds (Greenberg 1988, 93, 145).

Greenberg's book asks, "What price integration?" In describing the coming together of two different worlds through the perceptions of a man who has neither sight nor hearing, it treats us to a sociology of disabled people as colonial peoples and of the disabled experience as the colonial experience. John wavers between wanting integration into the world of the hearing and wanting the support and immediate, unconditional understanding and acceptance of the deaf-blind community. He resents the fact that the hearing world defines what is right and proper. He's quietly indignant when the director of the sheltered workshop tells him that his "deaf-blind" poetry won't sell because it offends. He feels shamed when the police treat him roughly and lock him up because of their incompetence to communicate with him or to understand who he is. He resents his lover's friends, who seem uninterested in him or his way of being, yet he's annoyed at his own friends for not accepting his relationship with his hearing, sighted lover. The book raises the question, can John live in both worlds? If his two worlds were to merge, would he lose his deaf-blind identity and perspective? Would it be subsumed by an insensitive hearing, sighted world?

Greenberg's *Small Differences* raises nearly the same questions as those that underpin this exploration of school inclusion. Can schools include people with disabilities in a way that values the person and yet does not ignore the effects of disability or the cultural experiences of people with disabilities?

CHAPTER VIII

Epilogue: Equality among Equals

THE EXPECTATION that people with disabilities and their families will fill a client role is widespread and relegates such people to special places and special treatments. Calling this perspective "smugness," Leonard Kriegel (1969, 423) recognizes its aim as distancing and isolating: "Smugness is the asset of the untouched, the virtue of the oblivious, and the badge of the unthreatened." Similarly, Bogdan and Taylor (1976), basing an article on the personal narratives of people labeled mentally retarded, titled it "The Judged, Not the Judges."

For the person classified disabled, the idea of being a client can become so overwhelming that he or she may come to believe it or at least accept it. For example, I recently asked a man who lives in the Danish institution Vangede whether he had any aspirations of getting out of the institution and into a job. He responded with a combination of sarcasm and impatience: "Haven't you seen that I am crippled?"

For those with disabilities the call to a client role—to be judged and treated—can be persistently heard nearly everywhere, at critical junctures in life (acceptance by a school, access to work, decisions about where and with whom to live) and in the most ordinary of situations and settings. In the category of the ordinary, a swim instructor apologized to Linda Till when he rejected Becky from his swim program: "We don't give therapy," he said. Linda Till responded chidingly, "Good. That's good, because I want her to learn swimming." The swim instructor saw her point: "Yeah, well that makes sense."

The idea pervades society that people must possess "special" skills to be around and to support a person with disabilities. Family friends wonder whether they can interact successfully with a child who does not speak or walk. They sometimes cast parents themselves in the role of special treatment experts, as the only people other than certified professionals who *can* support such children. Linda Till admits that she is disappointed when friends and organizations draw a circle around the family, treating Becky as someone who is tethered to specialists. Apparently, like regular class teachers, even friends worry that "they won't be able to meet her [Becky's] needs adequately and will cause her distress. I don't pretend that there aren't all kinds of needs that could cause her distress, but people *can* learn her care."

The Lehrs have commented on precisely the same phenomenon. On only three occasions has anyone stayed with Ben for several days without a family member present. Ben frequently has near-sleepless nights and when the Lehrs *have* gone away, the sleeplessness has ecalated. Bob and Sue believe that by not going away, they have probably contributed to Ben's difficulty in being separated from them, but they have seldom had the opportunity to leave him. And rarely has Ben been invited (alone, without other family members) for an outing. Bob Lehr longs for people to reach out to Ben naturally, of their own volition, not as a paid service: "I'd love to have people [say], 'I'm going to take [him] for the weekend. . . .' When it has that dimension, that makes me say, 'Somebody likes my kid.'"

Unwilling Clients

Transforming the "disabled" and their parents from perpetual clients to ordinary people requires more than an alteration in attitudes. It requires different conceptions of disability, of support, and of social settings.

It could be argued that schools serve the societal function of helping children and particularly youth to separate themselves from their parents and from the unconditional acceptance of the family. Schools, it might be said, are a transitional stage through which students enter the competitive "real world." But such explanations seem to justify a competitive ethic that marginalizes certain students or groups of students. They seem to legitimize discrimination and devaluation on the basis of the dominant society's preferences in matters of ability, gender, ethnicity, and race and to endorse an elaborate process of sorting by perceived ability and behavior. The parents in this study do not define schools or other social settings as *necessarily* heartless and rejecting. They envision schools as potentially welcoming and nurturing communities, inclusive rather than exclusive. In other words, the parents in this study would change institutional assumptions.

The events of Linda Till's Human Rights Commission appeal on Becky's behalf typify the parents' struggles. Before there could be a Human Rights Commission Board of Inquiry about Becky Till's claim to attend a regular class in a regular public school, the commission first had to decide whether the basis for a case existed. Consequently, a commission officer visited the Tills to investigate the claim. Toward the end of his day-long investigation, he said that the Tills would likely need a "current assessment of Becky to determine her particular needs." Linda rejected the idea immediately. He tried to convince her of the reasonableness of the request, but she would hear none of it. She reasoned that allowing an assessment would legitimate the notion that some children can be rightfully excluded from regular schools and regular classes, depending on the assessment's findings of their intellectual or physical abilities.

Linda Till had nothing against assessment if its purpose was to discover effective methods of education, but she would not allow its use as a means of denying Becky mainstream education: "The point at which they are ready to teach her and we are starting to plan for her, that's the point at which that information is relevant." Linda Till defended her "no preconditions" (that is, no prior assessment) stance on the presumption that Becky deserves ordinary status: "Becky is a child. She needs to go to school. And the school she needs to go to is her home school. Period." It wasn't that Becky did not have needs, but her needs were not all-defining of her as a person. "I don't want to get drawn into a discussion or dispute about is she or isn't she this degree or that degree of intellectual disability. Its not relevant to me and I don't want it to be relevant to them." Linda wanted expert help to be available to Becky but not help conditioned on the perception and treatment of her as other than an ordinary student.

Linda Till sought to reorder Becky's relationship to the professional world and therefore to society. This is essentially the main struggle of each of the parents featured in this book. And, frankly, Linda and the others often feel like lonely voices, themselves cast as disabled. Parents find that their own perspectives are discounted proportionately as professionals' ideas are elevated to "best method," "best practice," or "accepted practice" status. So long as professionals have the first and ultimate authority to define the best approach, parents stand below them in all debates over what to do for their children. Naturally then, many parents in the study are ambivalent about professionals.

The Lehrs often felt they were being seen as a bother. "We were always asking questions. We were always trying to find out what was going on. We were always looking over shoulders [of teachers]." Like the other parents, the Lehrs did not relish the role of pest. They had not volunteered for it. They would gladly have abandoned it. But they could not grant authority to anyone or any social institution that did not demonstrate an interest in Ben, an openness to learning about Ben, and a desire to discover ways of educating Ben that responded to Ben the person rather than to "Ben an autistic child."

Similarly, Rose Galati refuses to have Felicia put in with a "clump of kids, as many kids as . . . [the Board] could find—the mix of kids [with disabilities] is incredible—in a single high school."

Martha Jane Mason's son moved from a segregated special school into adult services four years before the writing of this book, yet she remained involved in political action to change public school policies. Recently, at a community meeting, several parents who are friends of hers spoke about their perception that school districts use special education to effect a racist segregation. One mother's account of her two boys' entrance into special education was particularly poignant:

> When my two boys were in first grade I was told they were gifted. They were given IQ tests and what not, and they [the school officials] told me they were thinking they were gifted. By the time they were in fourth grade, they were labeled emotionally disturbed. I could understand it maybe with one child. Maybe I could blame myself if one child had problems. But two? No, not two. I want to know what happened to my children. What happened to my two sons? Where did my two gifted sons go?

Other parents at the meeting had seen the same phenomenon; capable minority males were labeled by the schools as emotionally disturbed and effectively removed from the mainstream academic curriculum. A mother who works as a teacher's aide reported, "I see our kids being lost. They label them and they are lost. They are giving up on our kids. One ten-year-old boy told me this week that he'd like to kill himself because he can't read." Hearing this, a father in the meeting remarked, "I know we are smart. And I know our kids are smart. But they are not treated like they're smart." Another woman spoke with outrage of the school district's separate school for troublesome students, again predominantly minority and all male. She knows the school is a special school, purportedly for students with disabilities, but she calls it a jail. To these parents, special education is a process for removing certain students—who, they believe, are not disabled and who in fact may be very smart—from the regular schools. Their perspective does not really differ from that of the parents of children with obvious, severe, and multiple disabilities whose stories I have recounted in this book. In both situations, special education is a tool of discrimination.

Not surprisingly, students with disabilities find ways to show their displeasure at the rejection they encounter. They engage in a kind of negotiation with the world that sometimes only they seem to be aware of Catherine Woronko, for example, will lapse into self-stimulating rocking. Ben Lehr ignores people who are uncomfortable with him; he will leave the room, or he will simply announce, "No more." Last year he enjoyed attending an after-school teenagers' recreational program in the community. This year, with his favorite staff person gone and the program changed, Ben no longer attends. Ben remembers the names of people he likes; he calls out the names when the persons are absent, as if to say, "Come here; I want you with me" or "I'm thinking of you." For her part, Becky plays dumb when people treat her as if she is. She does the opposite when people show that they understand or want to understand what she might be thinking and feeling *and* that she is a feeling person.

The Wisdom of Allies

Chapter I described what happened when Rose Galati visited a school where a child asked why she did not live with her daughter, and Rose credits Maria's classmates in her first integrated class in Toronto with the support that enabled her to make the decision to bring Maria home. The students' actions touched Rose: They were "being nice to her and loving her. . . . If they can enjoy being with her, then can't we enjoy her just as much?"

The students had demonstrated the fundamental basis of equality, that people see each other as equally important, equally valuable. Much to their delight, Bob and Sue Lehr encountered this attitude of equal status at the Jowonio school. In their first meeting with the Jowonio staff, Ben was an invited participant: "They were very interested in having Ben be part of it. Questions were asked of Ben." Such a welcome was unexpected but cherished. Several years later, after Ben had entered an integrated public school, the Lehrs continued to hold up the Jowonio atmosphere as their ideal of the parent-professional relationship. To them, the most competent teachers were ones who always saw Ben as communicating something, even when he hurt himself or resisted an activity. The Jowonio teachers were open to Bob's and Sue's ideas and suggestions—

more evidence that they saw themselves as the Lehrs' peers, not as Ben's keeper or his parents' authority.

Bob Lehr defines competence as the ability to "be open . . . [to the fact] that you don't know everything. . . . And you can ask questions. And you can allow other people to participate." He says that with teachers, for example, it means having a relationship where "there is the feeling that we're not out to *get* the teacher, that when we do make suggestions we're just trying to make things better."

With each of these families, the principal mechanism for change is the example of their children. Their children are living texts. They are quiet, if sometimes unlikely, community educators and community organizers. Learning what she likes and doesn't like and how to transfer her from her wheelchair to a hammock, Maria Galati's classmates are evidence to her parents that integration is possible. The fact that Ben Lehr and Tommy Mason have always lived with their families and have not been sent to institutions suggests the possibility that other children with similar disabilities, including those who have a penchant for abusing themselves or who need basic hygienic care, can also stay in their home communities.

As this book goes to press, Martha Jane Mason is still struggling with her local social service agency to have two hours of home-aide services for Tommy, an hour each morning and each afternoon. For over four months this year, the agencies failed to provide the service. For the second time in two years, Mrs. Mason was forced to gather medical evidence concerning her heart condition and the extent to which it limits the direct care she can provide for Tommy. Despite these struggles and despite the absence of weekend or vacation respite services, Martha Jane declares that she will never allow Tommy to go to the institution, even if that is the only way for her to take a vacation.

Catherine Woronko is still enrolled in an integrated high school program. Mel Accetta and Maria Galati are attending their same schools and doing well. Felicia Galati and Ben Lehr have gone on to high school; their parents are still advocating better inclusion. Midway through Ben's first year of high school, the teachers and I introduced a way for him to communicate by typing. As a result, he has shown unexpected numeracy and literacy skills; in fact, he now takes high school biology and is earning passing grades. For the first time, moreover, he can express his feelings, ideas, and sense of humor. For the first time, teachers and parents do not need to guess his thoughts.

Meanwhile, although the Tills took Becky to the curb outside her local high school, accompanied by television cameras and news reporters, Becky was ignored. Public school officials would not integrate her. Finally, the Tills compromised and decided to send Becky to the local Catholic high school, where she *is* accepted. She is enrolled in regular ninth grade classes.

None of the changes needed to achieve integration is rooted in technique—for example, in getting a better diagnosis or even in finding a better method of education (although some people might contend that integrated schooling *is* a new and better method and that certain techniques such as Ben's typing make integration easier). Rather, these changes originate in a vision and a knowledge of people with disabilities as the equals of other people.

References

Asch, Adrienne 1989. "Has the Law Made a Difference? What Some Disabled Students Have to Say." In Dorothy K. Lipsky and Alan Gartner, eds., *Beyond Separate Education: Quality Education for All*, pp. 181–206. Baltimore, Md.: Paul H. Brookes.

Ashton-Warner, Sylvia. 1963. *Teacher*. New York: Simon & Schuster.

Bales v. Board of School Trustees, District 23 Central Okanagan. 1984.

Bates, Paul, Sue Ann Morrow, Ernie Pancsofar, and Robert Sedlak. 1984. "The Effect of Functional v. Nonfunctional Activities on Attitudes/Expectations of Non-Handicapped College Students: What They See Is What We Get." *Journal of the Association for Persons with Severe Handicaps* 9 (2): 73–78.

Biklen, Douglas. 1985. *Achieving the Complete School*. New York: Teachers College Press.

———. 1987. "In Pursuit of Integration." In M. S. Berres and Peter Knoblock, eds., *Program Models for Mainstreaming: Integrating Students with Moderate to Severe Disabilities*, pp. 19–40. Rockville, Md.: Aspen.

———. 1988. *In Support of Families*. Syracuse, N.Y.: Center on Human Policy, Syracuse University.

———. 1989. "Making Difference Ordinary: Strategies for Educating Students of Varying Abilities Together." In Susan Stainback, William Stainback, and Marsha Forest, eds., *Integrating Regular and Special Education*. Baltimore, Md.: Paul H. Brookes.

Biklen, Douglas, C. Corrigan, and D. Quick. 1989. "Beyond Obligation: Students' Relations with Each Other in Integrated Classes." In Dorothy K. Lipsky and Alan Gartner, eds., *Beyond Separate Education:*

189

Quality Education for All, pp. 207–22. Baltimore, Md.: Paul H. Brookes.

Blatt, Burton. 1966. *Christmas in Purgatory.* Boston: Allyn & Bacon.

———. 1970. *Exodus from Pandemonium: Human Abuse and a Reformation of Public Policy.* Boston: Allyn & Bacon.

———. 1972. Public Policy and the Education of Children with Special Needs. *Exceptional Children* 38:537–45.

———. 1973. *Souls in Extremis: An Anthology on Victims and Victimizers.* Boston: Allyn & Bacon.

———. 1977. Issues and Values. In Burton Blatt, Douglas Biklen, and Robert Bogdan, eds., *An Alternative Textbook in Special Education*, pp. 3–27. Denver: Love.

Board of Education of the Hendrick Hudson Central School District, Westchester County, et al., v. Amy Rowley. 1982. 458 U.S. 176.

Bogdan, Robert. 1980. "What Does It Mean When a Person Says, 'I Am Not Retarded'?" *Education and Training of the Mentally Retarded* 15(1): 74—79.

Bogdan, Robert, and Steven J. Taylor. 1976. "The Judged, Not the Judges: An Insider's View of Mental Retardation." *American Psychologist* 31 (1): 47–52.

———. 1987. "Toward a Sociology of Acceptance: The Other Side of the Study of Deviance." *Social Policy* 18:34–39.

Brinker, Richard, and M. Thorpe. 1984. Integration of Severely Handicapped Students and the Proportion of IEP Objectives Achieved. *Exceptional Children* 51:168–75.

Brown, Lou, Alison Ford, Jane Nisbet, Mark Sweet, Anne Donnellan, and Lee Gruenewald. 1983. "Opportunities Available When Severely Handicapped Students Attend Chronological Age Appropriate Regular Schools. *Journal of the Association for Persons with Severe Handicaps* 8 (1): 16–24.

Brown, Lou, Jane Nisbet, Alison Ford, Mark Sweet, Betsy Shiraga, Jennifer York, and Ruth Loomis. 1983. "The Critical Need for Nonschool Instruction in Educational Programs for Severely Handicapped Students." *Journal of the Association for Persons with Severe Handicaps* 8(3): 71–79.

Brown, Lou, Betsy Shiraga, Alison Ford, Jane Nisbet, Patricia VanDeventer, Mark Sweet, Jenifer York, and Ruth Loomis. 1986. "Teaching Severely Handicapped Students to Perform Meaningful Work in Nonsheltered Vocational Environments." In Richard J. Morris and Burton Blatt, eds., *Special Education: Research and Trends*, pp. 131–89. New York: Pergamon.

Buck v. Bell. 1927. 274 U.S. 200.

Carriere v. Lamond Board of Education. 1978. Alberta, Canada.

Charter of Rights and Freedoms. 1982. Ottawa, Canada.

Children's Defense Fund. 1974. *Children Out of School in America.* Washington, D.C.: Washington Research Project.

Coon, Marcey, R. Timm Vogelsberg, and Wes Williams. 1981. "Effects of Classroom Public Transportation Instruction on Generalization to the Natural Environment." *Journal of the Association for Persons with Severe Handicaps* 6 (2): 46–53.

Crossley, Rosemary, and Anne McDonald. 1980. *Annie's Coming Out.* New York: Penguin.

Cutler, Barbara C. 1981. *Unraveling the Special Education Maze.* Champaign, Ill.: Research Press.

Dahl, Roald. 1962. *James and the Giant Peach.* New York: Knopf.

Danielson, Lawrence G., and G. Thomas Bellamy. 1989. "State Variation in Placement of Children with Handicaps in Segregated Environments." *Exceptional Children* 55:448–55.

DES (Department of Education and Science). 1978. *Special Educational Needs: The Warnock Report.* London: HMSO.

Developmentally Disabled Assistance and Bill of Rights Act. 1975. 42 U.S.C.

Dexter, Lewis Anthony. 1962. "On the Politics and Sociology of Stupidity in Our Society." *Social Problems* 9:221–28.

Education Act. 1981. London: HMSO.

Featherstone, Helen. 1981. *A Difference in the Family.* New York: Penguin.

Forest, Marsha, ed. 1987. *More Education/Integration.* Downsview, Ont.: G. Allan Roeher Institute.

Freire, Paulo. 1970. *Pedagogy of the Oppressed.* New York: Herder & Herder.

Gould, Stephen J. 1981. *The Mismeasure of Man.* New York: Norton.

Greenberg, Joanne. 1988. *Of Such Small Differences.* New York: Henry Holt.

Groce, Nora. 1985. *Everyone Here Spoke Sign Language: Hereditary Deafness on Martha's Vineyard.* Cambridge, Mass.: Harvard University Press.

Halle, James. 1982. "Teaching Functional Language to the Handicapped: An Integrative Model of Natural Environment Teaching Techniques." *Journal of the Association for Persons with Severe Handicaps* 7 (4): 29–37.

Heller, Kirby A., Wayne H. Holtzman, and Samuel Messick, eds., 1982. *Placing Children in Special Education: A Strategy for Equity.* Washington, D.C.: National Academy Press.

Higgins, Paul. 1982. *Outsiders in a Hearing World*. Berkeley, Calif.: Sage.

Hunt, Pam, Lori Goetz, and Jacki Anderson. 1986. "The Quality of IEP Objectives Associated with Placement on Integrated versus Segregated School Sites." *Journal of the Association for Persons with Severe Handicaps* 11 (2): 125–30.

Kaye, Nancy. 1981. "Nancy Kaye." In William Roth, ed., *The Handicapped Speak*, pp. 49–69. Jefferson, N.C.: McFarland.

Kennedy, Margaret. 1964. *Not in the Calendar*. New York: Macmillan.

Knoblock, Peter. 1982. *Teaching and Mainstreaming Autistic Children*. Denver: Love.

Konrad, George. 1976. *The Case Worker*. New York: Bantam Books.

Kriegel, Leonard. 1969. "Uncle Tom and Tiny Tim: Some Reflections on the Cripple as Negro." *American Scholar* 38 (3): 412–30.

Kugel, Robert, and Wolf Wolfensberger, eds. 1969. *Changing Patterns in Residential Services for the Mentally Retarded*. Washington, D.C.: GPO.

Liberty, Katharine, Norris Haring, and Meredith Martin. 1981. "Teaching New Skills to the Severely Handicapped." *Journal of the Association for Persons with Severe Handicaps* 6 (1): 5–13.

Lipsky, Dorothy K., and Alan Gartner, eds., 1989. *Beyond Separate Education*. Baltimore, Md.: Paul H. Brookes.

McGee, John, Paul D. Menousek, and Daniel Hobbs. 1987. "Gentle Teaching: An Alternative to Punishment." In Steven J. Taylor, Douglas Biklen, and James Knoll, eds., *Community Integration for People with Severe Disabilities*, pp. 147–83. New York: Teachers College Press.

Magnetti, Suzanne S. 1982. "Some Potential Incentives of Special Education Funding Practices." In Kirby A. Heller, Wayne H. Holtzman, and Suzanne S. Messick, eds., *Placing Children in Special Education: A Strategy for Equity*, pp. 300–321. Washington, D.C.: National Academy Press.

Mairs, Nancy. 1986. *Plaintext: Deciphering a Woman's Life*. New York: Harper & Row.

Massie, Robert, and Suzanne S. Massie. 1976. *Journey*. New York: Warner Books.

Mathews, Gwyneth F. 1983. *Voices from the Shadows*. Toronto: Women's Educational Press.

Ministerial Review of Educational Services for the Disabled. 1984. *Integration in Victorian Education*. Melbourne: Ministry of Education.

Park, Clara C. 1967. *The Siege*. Boston: Little, Brown.

Perske, Robert. 1988. *Circles of Friends*. Nashville, Tenn.: Abingdon Press.

Pieper, Elizabeth. N.D. *Sticks and Stones*. Syracuse, N.Y.: Human Policy Press.

Public Law 94-142. 1975. *The Education for All Handicapped Children Act*, 20 U.S.C.

Rehabilitation Act. 1973. PL 93-112, 20 U.S.C.

Rivera, Geraldo. 1972. *Willowbrook: A Report*. New York: Vintage.

Rogers, Rick. 1986. *Caught in the Act: What LEA's Tell Parents under the 1981 Education Act*. London: Center for Studies on Integration in Education.

Roth, William. 1981. *The Handicapped Speak*. Jefferson, N.C.: McFarland.

Shearer, Ann. 1981. *Disability: Whose Handicap?* Oxford: Basil Blackwell.

Snow, Judith. 1988. Bradwyn Address, 89th annual meeting of Frontier College, Toronto, Ont.; reprinted in Marsha Forest with Bruce Kappel, eds. *It's About Learning*, pp. 143–49. Toronto: Frontier College Press.

Stainback, Susan, William Stainback, and Marsha Forest. 1989. *Integrating Regular and Special Education*. Baltimore, Md.: Paul H. Brookes.

Strully, Jeff, and Cindy Strully. 1985. "Friendship and Our Children." *Journal of the Association for Persons with Severe Handicaps* 10 (4): 224–27.

Taylor, Steven J. 1988. "Caught in the Continuum." *Journal of the Association for Persons with Severe Handicaps* 13 (1): 41–53.

Taylor, Steven J., Douglas Biklen, and James Knoll. 1987. *Community Integration of People with Severe Disabilities*. New York: Teachers College Press.

Taylor, Steven J., and Dianne Ferguson. 1985. "A Summary of Strategies Utilized in Model Programs and Resource Materials." In Susan Stainback and William Stainback, eds., *Integration of Students with Severe Handicaps into Regular Schools*, pp. 125–45. Reston, Va.: ERIC Clearinghouse on Handicapped and Gifted Children, Council for Exceptional Children.

Tomlinson, Sally. 1981. *Educational Subnormality: A Study in Decision-Making*. London: Routledge & Kegan Paul.

Towfighy-Hooshyar, Nahid, and Harvey Zingle. 1984. "Regular-Class Students' Attitudes toward Integrated Multiply Handicapped Peers." *American Journal of Mental Deficiency* 88:630–37.

U.S. Department of Education. 1985. *Seventh Annual Report to Congress on the Implementation of Public Law 94-142: The Education for All Handicapped Children Act*. Washington, D.C.: GPO.

———. 1986. *Eighth Annual Report to Congress on the Implementation of Public Law 94-142: The Education for All Handicapped Children Act.* Washington, D.C.: GPO.

———. 1988. *Tenth Annual Report to Congress on the Implementation of Public Law 94-142: The Education for All Handicapped Children Act.* Washington, D.C.: GPO.

Voeltz, Luanna. 1982. "Effects of Structured Interactions with Severely Handicapped Peers on Children's Attitudes." *American Journal of Mental Deficiency* 86:180–90.

———. 1984. "Program and Curriculum Innovations to Prepare Children for Integration." In N. Certo, N. Haring, and R. York, eds., *Public School Integration of Severely Handicapped Students*, pp. 155–84. Baltimore, Md.: Paul H. Brookes.

Wehman, Paul, M. Hill, P. Goodall, P. Cleveland, V. Brooks, and J. Pentecost. 1982. "Job Placement and Follow-up of Moderately and Severely Handicapped Individuals after Three Years." *Journal of the Association for Persons with Severe Handicaps* 7 (2): 5–16.

Wilcox, Barbara, and G. Thomas Bellamy. 1982. *Design of High School Programs for Severely Handicapped Students.* Baltimore, Md.: Paul H. Brookes.

Wolfensberger, Wolf. 1978. "The Ideal Human Service for a Societally Devalued Group." *Rehabilitation Literature* 39:(1): 15–17.

Worth, Patrick. 1988. "You've Got a Friend." In D. Gold and J. McGill, eds., *The Pursuit of Leisure*, pp. 47–52. Downsview, Ont.: G. Allan Roeher Institute.

Youngberg v. Romeo. 1982. 457 U.S. 307.

Ysseldyke, James, Bob Algozzine, Mark Shinn, and Mathew McAve. 1982. "Similarities and Differences between Low Achievers and Students Classified Learning Disabled." *Journal of Special Education* 16:73–84.

Index